# JIHAD ACADEMY

# JIHAD ACADEMY
## THE RISE OF ISLAMIC STATE

Nicolas Hénin

Translated from French by Martin Makinson

BLOOMSBURY

NEW DELHI • LONDON • OXFORD • NEW YORK • SYDNEY

ISBN 978 93 854 3603 1
2 4 6 8 10 9 7 5 3

Bloomsbury Publishing India Pvt. Ltd
DDA Complex, LSC Building No.4
Second Floor, Pocket C – 6 & 7, Vasant Kunj
New Delhi 110070
www.bloomsbury.com

Typeset by Manmohan Kumar
Printed and bound in India by Thomson Press India Ltd.

To find out more about our authors and books visit www.bloomsbury.com.
Here you will find extracts, author interviews, details of forthcoming
events and the option to sign up for our newsletters.

# Contents

# I Am Not Afraid

The reader may be surprised not to discover in the following pages the story of my captivity. Of course, I could have written the usual book describing my capture by masked Islamic State militants in a street of Raqqa, Syria, on 22 June 2013. I could have told of my ten months as a hostage alongside two dozen Westerners, including the Americans James Foley, Steven Sotloff, Peter Kassig and Kayla Mueller, Britons David Haines and Alan Henning, and Russian Sergei Gorbunov—all of them killed by their captors, who were also mine. I could have recounted the boredom, the fear and the suffering during the months I was deprived of my freedom, and finally my release in April 2014, after the negotiations conducted by my government. But the truth of the matter is that during these months I did not stop being a journalist.

Once free, I soon felt shocked—not by the cruelty of the ordeal I had undergone, but by the mistakes made by the entire international community, which had led the Middle East I love to such a momentous tragedy. I was stunned by the fact that these mistakes were being repeated again and again. When we fail to learn from history, even from the most immediate past, history exacts its revenge and returns to haunt us.

Telling only the standard tale of a casualty of terrorism, drawing the reader's attention to the ordeal endured, would have gone against my own beliefs. What I went through was a nightmare. Yet this nightmare is nothing compared to the scale of the tragedy being suffered by the people of Syria and Iraq. It is the great powers who have manufactured the conditions for this nightmare to come true, and who, at home, are creating the lost fanatics who willingly set off to fight in a war which is not theirs and whose issues they cannot grasp.

The world seems paralysed by fear of the people who took me hostage. These people are selling us a myth, in which they want to appear as super-terrorists, a new ultra-powerful generation. And we buy this myth. The world sees them as the very embodiment of evil and barbarity, wants to confront them, fight them. This is what Islamic State want, to drag the West on to its terrain. But I am not afraid. I know where these lost youths come from. I know their weaknesses. And I know above all how to deconstruct their myths, by draining the mire that produced them. This is what this book aims to do.

It was not accident, madness or provocation that made the US General David Petraeus express the view that 'Islamic State isn't our biggest problem in Iraq'.[1] He could have added it is not Syria's most unsolvable issue, even as he was explaining to me how he was 'profoundly worried about the continuing meltdown of Syria, which is a political Chernobyl. Until it is capped, it is going to continue to spew radioactive instability and extremist ideology in the entire region.'

Despite what I have endured, despite Islamic State's chilling deeds, I would like to invite people to assess this organisation in relative terms. I am not pursuing some kind of revisionism.

[1] Interview with Liz Sly, *Washington Post*, 20 March 2015.

I am saying it because first of all, in terms of terrorism, they have produced nothing fundamentally new or exceptional. And above all because putting their crimes in perspective enables us to do justice to the victims of *state* terrorism, who are ten times more numerous, and to remember that these jihadists who seek to spread fear among us are ultimately just a symptom, not a cause. They are only the fever. The disease is elsewhere.

I am not afraid, but I am worried. Worried about the future of a Middle East that still has a heavy price to pay for freedom. Worried about the world my children will inherit, in which terrorism feeds fear of Islam and xenophobia, in which the world's crises elicit only security responses from developed countries, and in which barriers and surveillance replace efforts to understand. Hence this book: the work of a journalist. To invite people to ponder, to think critically, to escape clichés and the all-too-easy solutions that flood our media.

Nicolas Hénin
Paris, May 2015

# Introduction

The hills of Raqqa in the Euphrates valley, with their parched, stony gorges, achieved notoriety one fateful morning in August 2014. A video was posted online: the picture faded in to reveal a hostage in an orange jumpsuit and his taunting executioner brandishing a knife. A short harangue, a final provocation, and a last message from the victim to his family. Then one more murder under the Syrian sun.

James Foley's macabre execution was successful beyond its perpetrators' dreams. The West was stunned. The summer holidays were over. Obama held a crisis meeting and Cameron cut short his holidays. After three years of waiting, inaction and procrastination, violence suddenly invaded our screens and forced us to react. Islamic State had thrust itself onto the agenda.

Yet we had seen Islamic State coming, since its reasonably amicable split from al-Qaida's official franchise in Syria, Jabhat al-Nusra. Islamic State has made relentless advances amid rampaging violence, rifts amid the Syrian opposition to the regime, and growing despair and frustration. Its progress seemed to halt in the spring, as armed groups in Syria engaged in internecine battles, but the deteriorating situation in Iraq gave it fresh momentum. Islamic State took Mosul almost without a shot being fired and established a caliphate. Or rather it restored a caliphate that had existed, uninterrupted, throughout Islamic history until 1924.

It was as if, with the murder in the Syrian desert, we had suddenly become aware of the challenge we faced from Syria, Iraq and the group that calls itself Islamic State.[1] There had already been thousands, even hundreds of thousands of deaths. But this particular death grabbed our attention. It affected us directly. This was no longer Syrians murdering Syrians, it was not just an Arab affair. These were our people. In the midst of the Syrian civil war, an American from New Hampshire had been killed in cold blood by a British national from East London.

For the last three years, in the Syrian crisis alone, the damage has been extensive. Half a million people have been seriously injured. Two hundred thousand are missing, fighters or civilians in detention, subjected to torture, people who may never return. At least a third of homes have been damaged; nearly half of all Syrians have had to leave theirs. As refugees or displaced people, they are crammed into insecure camps. But the psychological damage is even more severe and will be harder to repair. It is difficult to imagine how the different components of Syrian society can be put back together after such an outpouring of hatred and violence.

---

[1] Islamic State (called Islamic State in Iraq and the Levant, or ISIL, until June 2014, when it shed any reference to territory) is known by several names. Anglo-American sources generally use the initials 'IS', 'ISIS' or 'ISIL'. In France and in the Middle East it is often called by its Arabic acronym Daesh, but when spoken this name has a very pejorative association. Much of the media have decided to add the word 'group' to its name, to stress that it is not a real state. I consider that I should use not any other name than the one it uses itself; I'd prefer to focus my critique on its actions and ideology rather than resort to anathema. The term 'Islamic State' will be used in this book unless people quoted or interviewed use a different one.

Iraqi society can take no more upheavals. In thirty-five years, it has experienced a terrible war against Iran, destructive international intervention followed by a criminal regime of sanctions, a further invasion and the horrors of a poorly concluded occupation. When the invader packs his bags, he nearly always leaves crucial issues unresolved.

In 2011, the departure of the last American troops paradoxically initiated a new period of instability, under the leadership of the highly authoritarian and sectarian Prime Minister Nouri al-Maliki. As a result, in much of Iraq, US occupation was replaced by a much more insidious phenomenon— *self*-occupation by the country's own security forces. It was strange to see Iraqi soldiers manning checkpoints on Iraq's roads and patrolling city streets, looking arrogantly down on the Iraqi population and mimicking the attitude of their US predecessors.

Islamic State's rise has been made possible by a mix of discrimination, marginalisation and sectarianism. In the West, it has provided an opportunity to youths suffering from an identity crisis who want a way to express their revolt against injustice and society's contradictions. In Syria and Iraq, it has festered among populations subjected to violence and deprived of hope. The breakdown of these states has created a space in which Islamic State can flourish.

The challenges posed by this crisis are new and require a comprehensive response. A reaction based solely on policing, legal measures and intelligence is doomed to fail. Likewise, a military operation, regardless of the means mobilised, can only spell disaster, since the intervention of ground troops (except for the discreet efforts of special forces) is out of the question, as there is no support for it. When the frustration of a youth from the European suburbs combines with the rage of a Syrian persecuted by his own country's security forces, it's easy to understand why public agencies need to work together. Diplomatic efforts must apply pressure to bring about political transition in the states concerned. Humanitarian organisations need to act, because there is no better breeding ground for extremism than entire populations in despair.

It will be no easy task. Competing powers are involved in the crisis in Syria and Iraq, each hoping to strengthen its own position. The Russian–Iranian axis believes its survival is at stake. For the Gulf monarchies, it provides a way of containing the 'Shia Crescent' while strengthening the conservative tendencies within the Arab Spring. Turkey, having had to abandon its good-neighbour diplomatic policy, is now trying to suppress Kurdish claims at the same time as containing the jihadist thrust. But Turkey does not understand that the countries in the region don't look favourably on its neo-Ottoman imperialism. Finally, the West, as so often, views the crisis in terms of security, and has a particular fixation on Israel; it remains entangled in contradictions over the vital issues of human rights and the protection of civilians.

It was in the Tigris and Euphrates valleys that writing, literature, mathematics, law and trade were invented. It was here that the foundations of medicine and philosophy were laid. And here too that humans banded together to tame nature, and so learned to live in society, and invented the foundations of the state and government.

During my months of captivity in Islamic State's cellars, I often revisited Berlin's Pergamon Museum in my mind. With my eyes closed, I visualised the Ishtar Gate, fragments of the *Epic of Gilgamesh*, the tablets and small scrolls on which the most ancient extant traces of writing are inscribed. And the splendid Aleppo Room! I also remembered my visit two years earlier to the Ziggurat of Ur in southern Iraq, and my report from the house of Abraham, clumsily reconstructed by Saddam Hussein. My mind was constantly full of memories of the Sumerian, Hittite, Babylonian and Assyrian cultures, as well as the Abbasid and Umayyad Caliphates, so different in their enlightenment from that of the sinister Ibrahim. What a brutal contrast between the obscene reality I was experiencing and the riches of these civilisations in the pages of our shared history.

But we need to remember what these jihadists have forgotten, what even the leaders in the region who are blithely obliterating their heritage have forgotten: Iraq and Syria are the cradle of our civilisation. Our roots are being destroyed in this conflict, too.

If that world collapses, ours is threatened.

# 1

# Marketing Secularism

*The Syrian regime is not secular. Its foundations are built on sectarianism. Its claim to defend minorities is a myth.*

For over four decades, Syria has been ruled by an authoritarian regime run by the Ba'ath ('rebirth') party, whose motto 'Unity, freedom, socialism' initially sounded promising. The Ba'ath movement was founded near the end of the Second World War by a Sunni (Salah ad-Din Bittar), an Alawi (Zaki al-Arsouzi) and a Christian (Michel Aflak); it defined itself as pan-Arab and revolutionary and came into being in a context of decolonisation and debates over Third World non-alignment during the Cold War. Given its declared commitment to economic self-sufficiency, education and women's emancipation, and resolute opposition to political Islam, it could have set Syria on the path to prosperity for all its citizens.

But none of this took account of Hafez al-Assad's personality. He was the architect of a coup in 1970. He established a pyramidal leadership structure and system of allegiance: at the top were the president and his family; next, his clan; below them, his community, the Alawis, considered a branch of Shia Islam since colonial days; and, right at the bottom, the rest of the population.

Today, faced with a majority-led insurgency, this regime emphasises its secularism and sets itself up as sole defender of minorities. It trots out this script endlessly, like a commercial slogan. 'The fall of the Syrian regime would mean the elimination of the region's minorities,' one of its apologists, the French-Lebanese MP Nabil Nicolas, insisted on Hezbollah's TV channel, al-Manar, on 23 May 2011. Bouthaina Shaaban, media adviser to Syria's president, even tried to sell the idea of a plot against secularism in the Arab world. Maintaining that there were still three secular countries in the region (Sudan, Iraq and Syria), she expressed regret at the division of Sudan into South and North, the invasion of Iraq and 'aggression' against Syria. She complained that 'Western states and their regional allies are seeking to destroy the secular regime in Syria,'[1] a piece of propaganda which struck a chord from the anti-globalisation far left to an extreme right preoccupied with identity issues, *de facto* creating a repugnant coalition of anti-Semites and Islamophobes. The French Internet site *Riposte Laïque*, which has close links with the far right, was only too happy to publish the half-baked ideas of Hamdan Ammar, who claimed 'the Americans want to redraw the geostrategic map of the region at any cost. Having handed Iraq to the Shias, they are now trying to cause Syria to fall into Sunni hands. It's a dangerous game they're playing.'[2]

This promotion of the idea of a Syrian regime that defends its Christians is carefully stage-managed. Any visit from an academic, MP, lobbyist with the potential to involve Syria's Christian groups is always seized upon and exploited in news reports.

[1] Quoted by the Russian press agency RIA Novosti, 19 June 2012.

[2] http://ripostelaique.com/que-se-passe-t-il-reellement-en-syrie.html.

Soon after the Ba'ath party came to power, its relationship with the Sunni majority turned sour. Very quickly, the regime targeted the Muslim Brotherhood, one of the only forces which could claim to constitute any sort of opposition. The Brotherhood was banned in 1964. The army suppressed strikes and demonstrations in the years that followed. But it was the assumption of power by Hafez al-Assad in 1970 and, in particular, the Syrian invasion of Lebanon in 1976, that lit the touch paper. Confrontation escalated: there were terrorist attacks and murders on one side, and arrests and torture on the other. Then, in 1979, a sectarian offshoot of the Brotherhood launched an attack against the Aleppo artillery academy. Eighty-three cadets, all Alawis, were killed. The regime's revenge was ruthless. A full-scale civil war followed, which was little known in the West since no media were able to cover it. It ended with the crushing of the city of Hama in 1982. Tens of thousands of people were killed. Thousands more were deported to the Palmyra prison in the middle of the eastern desert, which effectively became an extermination camp. This massacre—which sparked little international protest—brought the regime three decades of relative internal peace, at a high price. The regime sent a number of Christian officers to the front line to crush the Hama insurgency. This was a Machiavellian way of sealing a blood pact with the Christian community. The message was clear: if one day the Sunni are in a position to take their revenge, they will avenge themselves on you as much as on us. Your fate now depends on our regime's survival.

When Bashar al-Assad assumed power after his father's death in 2000, there were hopes the regime would begin evolving towards greater secularism founded on religious tolerance. Relations with the opposition improved significantly. Many members of the Brotherhood were released from prison and its exiled political leadership in London announced a change in policy, rejecting violence and calling for a modern, democratic state. Simultaneously, the country opened up both politically and economically. Discussion forums sprang up. This period, known as the 'Damascus Spring', aroused great hopes. Yet disappointment swiftly followed this precursor of the Arab Spring. The regime soon reverted to its obsession with security and old habits were resumed. Most of the leaders of this political renewal—intellectuals, lawyers and rebel MPs— were arrested and imprisoned. The regime had shown its intrinsic inability to reform.

Ayman Abdel-Nour, a Syrian dissident, journalist and ex-Ba'athist, knew Assad well. They were close at university and subsequently remained good friends: Abdel-Nour had helped Assad in the early years of his presidency. Now he is a particularly well-informed critic who runs All4Syria.info, one of the main sources of independent information on Syria. Ayman Abdel-Nour is himself a Christian. His relations with the regime became so bad that he had to go into exile in the Gulf. In an interview with *Souriya ala toul*, he describes the fallacy of Assad's 'secularism':

> From the first day, the regime pressed sectarian buttons, even before there was any Islamic dimension, Islamic slogans, or Islamic movement. ... He managed to terrorise Christians living inside and outside Syria ... The regime has been unrelenting in its attempts to divide religious communities in every possible way. It has worked hard at reducing their clout by giving artificial importance to others, people created by the regime itself and who were therefore linked to it and owed it something.[3]

---

[3] Published by All4Syria, 13 October 2013.

Behind its façade of secularism, the Syrian regime has built a survival mechanism that presents a form of communalism based on the concept of *assabiyat* (tribal solidarity or clan spirit) which has been well described by Michel Seurat, an experienced observer of what he called 'a state of barbarity'.[4] Seurat's critique cost him his life, since Damascus expressly requested his Hezbollah kidnappers to ensure his death. More recently, the scholar Zakaria Taha, also interested in Assad junior, focused his PhD dissertation on 'understanding how these regimes manage to recast themselves in the image of a secular power, while manipulating communities and transforming secularism into a tool to legitimise and perpetuate their rule under the pretext of fighting sectarian divisions and working for national unity.'[5]

It is all about marketing and presentation. As sociologist Burhan Ghalioun has pointed out, an examination of the facts reveals that this Syrian-style secularism 'tends to become a source of justification or inspiration for the censorship of consciences, for ideological intolerance and even for the rejection of the principle of democracy ...'[6] 'The secularism card,' Zakaria Taha concludes, 'is the only one left to play for a regime that presents itself to minorities as the bulwark against all conflict.'[7]

'The regime uses secularism as an instrument, as something it can sell to the West,' says Yassin al-Haj Saleh, a Raqqa

[4] Michel Seurat, *Syrie, l'état de barbarie*, PUF (reprint, not translated into English), 2012.

[5] Zakariah Taha, *La problématique de la laïcité à travers l'expérience du parti Baath en Syrie*, EHESS, 2012,

[6] Burhan Ghalioun, *Islam et politique, la modernité trahie*, La Découverte, 1997.

[7] Zakariah Taha, *La problématique de la laïcité à travers l'expérience du parti Baath en Syrie*, EHESS, 2012.

intellectual and one of the first communist opponents of the regime. 'I believe it has given a lot of money to public relations firms to sell its supposed modernity, particularly by making use of the image of Asma, the first lady who is beautiful and British-educated. But ultimately, we are dealing with two kinds of fascists: the ones in the government who wear ties and the ones with long beards. But our struggle must not be limited to taking a position between these two types of fascism.'

In reality, the regime feeds sectarian fears. It did, after all, claim when the revolution began, that the demonstrators were chanting: 'Christians to Beirut, Alawis to the grave!' ('*Massihiyin bi-Beirut, Alawiyin bi-Tabut!*')

I have not found any confirmation of this claim. Yet many people believed the threat was real and from the start of the uprising it contributed to inter-communal tension. Also early on, the regime distributed weapons, particularly in the Alawi coastal villages and the Druze suburbs of Damascus, and these deliveries were accompanied by scaremongering about entirely invented threats, said to originate in neighbouring Sunni villages.

Yassin al-Haj Saleh is an old communist militant from Raqqa, long opposed to the regime. These Machiavellian tactics do not surprise him in the least. In a chilling article 'The Murder Industry in Syria'[8] he describes Assad's methods of creating two walls of fear: fear of oppression by the regime and the fear of potential informants: 'Before the outbreak of the revolution, we knew the regime depended on two Orwellian strategic systems: the fear complex, whose aim is to prevent things being called by their proper names, and the lie complex, whose function is to call things by other names than their own. Both ensure that

[8] Published in French by the weekly *L'Express*, 14 March 2014.

Syrians are cut off from the real conditions of their lives, and that they can neither describe nor control them.'

'From the beginning, the regime focused on the support of minorities. It gave them the highest positions in the army and intelligence services, knowing that in Syria you have to distinguish between job title and effective power,' Ayman Abdel-Nour, the founder of All4Syria explains. His website provides a platform for many representatives of Syrian minorities, where they can take the regime's narrative apart.

For example, when Bashar al-Assad dared to claim on the satellite channel Russia Today that his regime is 'the last fortress of secularism' in the Middle East, the Druze journalist Maher Sharafeddin responded on the All4Syria website with a series of questions, which is also a potent list of grievances:

1. Why does the defection of an ordinary Alawi citizen undermine the foundations of your regime more than that of a high-ranking officer, for example, a general from any other religious community?

2. Why do Hezbollah and the *Jaysh al-Mahdi* (Iraq's Mahdi army, founded by Muqtada al-Sadr) rush to the rescue of your 'secular' regime, when they are among the movements most violently opposed to secularism?

3. Why has the defection of the Prime Minister [Riyad Hijab] not provoked the slightest reaction at the top of the regime, while anywhere else such an event might have led to regime collapse?

4. Why did the victims of the explosion of the Alawi neighbourhood Mezzeh 86 in Damascus receive compensation, but not the inhabitants of other neighbourhoods subjected to attacks?

5. Why did your 'secularist' regime kidnap the (Alawi) dissident Abdel-Aziz al-Khayyer, when his demands are

so mild that other Syrian dissidents in Cairo once pelted him with eggs because of them?

6. Why have your media conducted such a massive and concerted smear campaign against the (Alawi) actress Fadia Suleyman, although she is just a peaceful artist who would be totally unable to handle a weapon even if she wanted to?

7. Why did you appoint a Christian defence minister after the outbreak of the revolution, and why did you discreetly tell your media which religious community he belongs to?

8. Why do your 'secular' regime's media focus mainly on terrorist attacks committed in regions inhabited by 'minorities'?

9. Why has your regime not killed a single demonstrator in Suwaida and Salamiya, which are respectively Druze and Ismaili strongholds, and has limited itself to frightening its opponents there by jailing a few of them, while elsewhere live ammunition has been used on demonstrators?

10. Why were the only neighbourhoods which avoided destruction in Homs those inhabited by people from your religious community?

11. Why has the regime of Nouri al-Maliki, who maintains he is 'Shia before Iraqi', become an essential ally of your 'secular' regime?

12. Why do Sunnis make up 99.99 per cent of those killed by your 'secular' army?

You can, if you wish, treat these questions as a test of secularism and intelligence.'

Thomas Pierret, a lecturer in Contemporary Islam at Edinburgh University, is surprised that the regime has in fact made so little of its secularism. Assad himself uses this term only in exceptional circumstances: when interviewed by Charlie Rose on PBS, he stated that his great challenge was to 'keep society as secular as it is today'. The president is shrewd enough to leave the topic of secularism to those he considers to be 'vulnerable fall guys, devoid of any credibility'; the Great Mufti Ahmad Hassoun, for instance. Pierret is interested in 'the presentation of the regime's *non-secularism*.'

In November 2011, for example, when welcoming the members of the Congregation of Ulema of Lebanon (a pro-Iranian organisation), Assad openly expressed regret over his past anti-religious policies and emphasised the government's recent launch of Nour al-Sham, an Islamic satellite channel. Pierret concludes that 'if the regime is indeed "secular", it's in a negative way, though it mobilises religious references extremely sparingly compared to the other regimes in the region.'

The number of its victims gives the lie to the regime's alleged 'protection of minorities'. Photographs secretly sent out by someone using the codename 'Caesar' are one of the best sources we have for cataloguing these crimes. 'Caesar', whose real identity remains secret, was employed by military police in Damascus; even before the revolution he was entrusted with photographing people killed (accidentally or deliberately) in events involving defence ministry staff. So for years he has seen the large numbers of detainees killed during repression, in Damascus's two military hospitals, Tishrine and Mezzeh. The bodies he photographed came from twenty-four centres under the supervision of the security services of the city's governorate. Nearly all the corpses showed signs of torture.

More than two years after the revolution began, he managed to send 55,000 pictures out of the country, documenting the fate of nearly 11,000 victims. These pictures prove in disturbing detail that the regime has indeed attacked minorities. Many Christians could be identified by the fact they were uncircumcised and by tattoos in the shape of the cross. Other victims bore religious markings indicating they were Shia, and others even had the name or face of Bashar al-Assad on their bodies.

The ability to instil terror in all religious communities, spreading it through all strata of society, has enabled the regime to maintain a wall of fear since coming to power. Alawi and Christian revolutionaries I met in Lattakia at the start of the uprising told me: 'God help us if the *Mukhabarat* [the dreaded intelligence services] catch us because they take it out on people like us in particular, because they consider us traitors to our community.'

So this is secularism, Assad-style. The first revolutionaries were very conscious of the trap set by the regime. Every week they voted online to name the following Friday's demonstration. Every demonstration had a new theme. There was the 'Friday of dignity', 'of martyrs' and 'of free women'. They had agreed to call the day of action in Easter week 'Good Friday'.

What the Syrian regime is really trying to impose is a form of political *dhimmi*-status on its minorities. In Islamic lands, the *dhimmi* is an unbeliever to whom the Muslim state extends protection in exchange for a tax called the *jizya*. In Assad's Syria, minorities are told to keep quiet, to toe the line politically if they want to preserve their security.

As Ayman Abdel-Nour sees it, 'the regime has always had a stable relationship with the Christians. It can be described as a bargain of sorts. In exchange for giving up political and economic rights, clergy members enjoy full religious rights.' The journalist, himself a Christian, considers that 'the Syrian Christian clergy has literally been bought wholesale by the regime. Churches receive free water and electricity. The clergy are spared military service. They have the right to purchase cars tax free, which requires the president's signature. So priests and bishops have to go to the palace to get permission to drive nice cars—and they all rush to do so.

'In the photos of every official event, there is always a representative of each religious denomination around the government representative. The regime has turned it into a competition between the representatives of each Christian church, who fight each other for the privilege of being in the photo. And there is also direct corruption, with cash handouts. I have no respect for the clergy in Syria!'

# 2

# Birth of the Jihadists

*The Syrian regime is not fighting Islamic State; it created it.*
*Islamic State in turn is not fighting the Syrian regime.*

The Syrian regime does not balk at contradictions when its own survival is at stake. Within Syria, it brutally represses the Muslim Brotherhood. But this is the better to outflank them, whereas it supports Islamist movements in neighbouring countries: Hamas in the Palestinian territories (itself a branch of the Muslim Brotherhood which does not balk at contradictions when under Assad's protection) and Hezbollah in Lebanon. Moreover, Syria has above all backed and patently manipulated two jihadi Salafist movements: the volunteers who went to Iraq to fight the US, at least during the early years of occupation, and the Fatah al-Islam in Lebanon.

When invasion was imminent in the winter of 2002–03, Saddam Hussein invited any Muslim who wished to do so, to come and defend Iraq, in particular against US forces. Several hundred fighters answered the call and converged mainly on Baghdad, a fact that itself defied rational explanation. Saddam's Iraq was Ba'athist and claimed to be secular, even if this secular front concealed a form of sectarianism similar to Syria's. Assad, whose wish to disrupt American plans was even stronger than his hatred of Saddam, allowed fighters to pass through his territory.

This influx of jihadists, the first in the Syrian-Iraqi region, went on unabated after the US invasion of March and April 2003. It put a 'jihad highway' on the map, through a territory that unsurprisingly matches Islamic State's current zone of influence.

I met several of these jihadists between 2002 and 2004, when I was a Middle East correspondent based in Baghdad. Later, while covering the Syrian revolution, I met the veterans of this insurgency again. They all described a broadly similar journey. The meeting point was usually a guesthouse linked to a mosque in Aleppo. From there, they would take a bus along the Euphrates valley, pass through Raqqa and Deir ez-Zor and arrive at Abu Kamal. From there, intermediaries could easily smuggle them across the Iraqi border. They travelled on via al-Qaim, Haditha and south to Falluja. Many stopped in the western province of Al Anbar. Those who went on to Baghdad would be lodged around Abu Ghraib or in the Amariyah district.

One of the organisers of this 'jihad highway' was Sheikh Mahmoud Abu al-Qaqa,[1] a young imam from Aleppo known for his inflammatory sermons inciting people to take up arms against the American invader. These public sermons were also distributed on cassettes and CDs which have been found among the possessions of many jihadists. The sheikh also called for an Islamic regime under Sharia law in Syria. Observers of politics in Aleppo followed the sheikh's development closely. He quite openly put up mujahadin in his own home before they left for Iraq. This provoked no reaction from the authorities, though Syrian intelligence agencies are usually very quick to identify and punish anything they consider irregular.

---

[1] His real name is Mahmoud Ghul Aghassi. He is a Kurdish religious sheikh from Aleppo.

The reason for this tolerance became clear only later: some of Abu al-Qaqa's young recruits never reached Iraq. Certainly none made it back alive. The imam was in fact what intelligence services call a 'honey pot', a lure to help identify candidates for jihad. They would leave for Iraq as marked men. Some would cross over; some probably died before they even set off. What mattered was that they were eliminated and never returned. And too bad if in the process some weak-minded people crossed the line into criminal activity. The sheikh was eventually shot dead in the street as he left a mosque after Friday prayers. Was this the *Mukhabarat* eliminating proof because people had begun to suspect the authorities' trap, or was it revenge by a jihadi who had been double-crossed? I don't know anyone who can answer this question. But in the light of recent events, it is disturbing to reread this assertion from an interview Abu al-Qaqa gave an American journalist a year before his assassination: 'Yes, I would like to see an Islamic state in Syria. That's what we are working for. We are calling for unity and understanding, and the government is part of that. We are calling for, and working with, the government to cooperate to that end.'[2] Abu al-Qaqa's mission was to identify potential jihadists, try to confirm their violent tendencies and then pass on their names to the authorities. The regime was killing two birds with one stone: it was getting rid of potentially violent youths to prevent them from taking action in Syria, and also using them as tools in a policy of destabilisation in Iraq. The same kind of reasoning—which is not only immoral but also ineffective from a security viewpoint—can also be found in France, where some people are happy to see young Frenchmen

[2] http://now.mmedia.me/lb/en/commentaryanalysis/death_of_a_cleric

go off to jihad. They greet their *hijra*[3] with repugnant cheers of 'good riddance!'

In Lebanon, the Syrian regime has supported jihadists through the Fatah al-Islam group. This group has been particularly active in the Nahr al-Bared refugee camp near Tripoli, in the north of the country. Here there were violent clashes between the movement and the Lebanese army in the summer of 2007, in the course of which the camp was set on fire and more than 200 people died (including 134 Lebanese soldiers).

According to Thomas Pierret, the aim was:

> To maintain a state of chaos in Lebanon under Fuad Siniora's administration, which is seen as a source of destabilisation for the Syrian regime, and to hit the *Al-Mustaqbal* party ['Future'] in its weakest spot, i.e. the radical Sunni base. *Al-Mustaqbal* (unlike Hezbollah, which is a revolutionary party that has been successful in mobilising and infiltrating the Shia community and uniting the pious middle class and poor youth, to use Gilles Kepel's terms) is a party of prominent figures which can only maintain the loyalty of the impoverished Sunni base through cronyism. By encouraging the emergence of a radical Sunni movement openly hostile to the pro-western posturing of *al-Mustaqbal* (while simultaneously being strangely silent about its enemies, namely Hezbollah, Iran and Syria), Damascus forced the Siniora government to go to war with part of its notional grassroots. At the time, Hezbollah's views on Fatah al-Islam had little to do with its current 'anti-takfiri' rhetoric. Hezbollah was delighted to

---

[3] Emigration to Muslim lands. This is the term used in particular to designate departure towards lands subjected to their notion of 'jihad'.

see its political opponents in difficulty, describing the army's entry in a Palestinian refugee camp as a 'red line', and refusing to call army casualties 'martyrs', as the rest of the Lebanese media were doing at the time.

Very soon after the revolution began, as people began to take up arms and the regime realised that the uprising was not just a passing phenomenon but a profound crisis capable of causing its downfall, Damascus began to exert pressure on democrats by favouring radicals.

'At the start of the revolution, I was invited to speak at a martyr's funeral,' the ex-MP and opposition figure Riad Seif told me. 'I warned against two traps Assad would lay: recourse to arms and sectarian war. And even then, I had not seen al-Qaida coming!'

The technique is a classic one seen in many previous conflicts. The Russians backed the Islamists within the Chechen guerrillas to cause them to split apart. The Israelis have long allowed Hamas to prosper with the hope of weakening the Palestine Liberation Organisation. Even Hafez al-Assad himself had outflanked the Islamists by outmanoeuvring them to their right and allowing the activities of extremely conservative but non-jihadi Salafists, who promoted 'quietism' to counter the Muslim Brotherhood's influence.

From the summer of 2011, detainees held for their alleged jihadi activities began to be released. In all, there were more than a thousand of them, and it seems that many of the current upper echelons of the hardline fundamentalist groups benefited from this amnesty. Abu Mohammad al-Julani, the leader of Jabhat al-Nusra—al-Qaida's official franchise in Syria—may have been among these released prisoners. Aaron Lund, editor of the website *Syria in Crisis*, thinks 'the regime has done a good job of turning the revolution into an Islamist revolution. The releases from Saidnaya prison (50 km north of Damascus), which is one of the main political prisons in central Syria, are a good example of this. Assad was able to claim these early releases were part of a general amnesty. But it seems to have gone much further than that. This regime does not carry out random acts of kindness.'[4]

In January 2014, Nawaf al-Fares, a former chief in Military Intelligence (*Amn al-Askari*), one of the many Syrian intelligence services, gave a sensational interview. Having deserted after twelve years in the secret service apparatus, he revealed that 'the regime did not just open the door to the prisons and let these extremists out; it facilitated them in their work, by helping them set up armed units.'

This four-month release programme was supervised by the Directorate of General Security and lasted until October 2011. The prisoners were carefully selected. Those with a known commitment to human rights and democracy remained in jail, while the radicals went free. One of the most famous was Zahran Alloush, who founded the most powerful anti-Assad group in the Damascus area as soon as he was freed and became well known for his violently anti-Shia rhetoric.

The *Daily Telegraph* quoted this former agent as saying 'the regime wanted to tell the world it was fighting al-Qaeda but in fact the revolution was peaceful in the beginning, so it had to create an armed Islamic revolt. There were strong Islamic tendencies to the uprising, so it was easy just to encourage them […]. You release just a few people and you create the violence. It will then spread by contagion.'

---

[4] Ruth Sherlock, 'Syria's Assad accused of boosting al-Qaida with secret oil deals', *Daily Telegraph*, 20 January 2014.

Major General Fayez Dwairi, the Jordanian army officer in charge of fighting the spread of jihadi ideology in his country, has confirmed this: 'Many of the people who created Jabhat al-Nusra were captured by the regime in 2008 and had remained in prison. When the revolution began, they were released on the order of Syrian intelligence officers, who told Assad: "They'll do good work for us. There are of course many drawbacks to letting them go, but there are even more advantages, because they'll convince the world that we are fighting Islamic terrorism."'[5] An additional factor, as pointed to by American scholar Joshua Landis and others, is that Syrian jihadist groups (particularly Islamic State) have been infiltrated by the regime's intelligence services. Also worth quoting is this admission by Abdullah Abu Mussab al-Souri, Omar al-Shishani's assistant: 'Of course Islamic State has been widely infiltrated by the Syrian regime, and this has weakened its position and jeopardised its security.'[6]

The political benefit for Damascus is obvious. It helps water down the narrative generally accepted by the Western media. Syria's revolution is no longer legitimate, it is a war against terror and a fanatical, sectarian enemy within that has now found legitimacy. In the worst-case scenario, if Syria comes to the brink of collapse, it will always be possible to sell the world 'the theory of the lesser evil', which presents the regime as less of a threat than Islamic State. The Assad family has always manipulated the 'me or chaos' slogan very persuasively. The jihadist bogeyman is shockingly effective.

This is why the regime will never strike the jihadists directly, but instead concentrate its military operations on those it

---

[5] Ibid.
[6] http://www.sada.pro/?p=18280

sees as presenting the greatest danger, the moderates who legitimately claim to represent a political alternative. The Free Syrian Army battalions and the democratic Islamist brigades have often manned the front line alone against the Syrian army. Even worse, they have been caught in the crossfire between the regime and Islamic State.

For the regime, this was the second advantage of Islamic State encroaching on, and then seizing, parts of Syria from the summer of 2014 onwards. Wherever Islamic State fighters advanced, they drove back moderate groups, forcing them from their hard-won territories. Islamic State is like a cuckoo, plundering the nest the revolutionaries fought so hard for. Almost all of the territory ruled by Islamic State was previously occupied by other groups. Islamic State has on the whole been content with seizing territory only after others have taken it.

As a result, Islamic State has rarely launched frontal attacks on the regime. To nip counter-arguments in the bud, let me list the exceptions. Islamic State fought the Syrian army when they seized the Menagh air base and when they captured Division 17 in Raqqa along with the neighbouring military airport. It also took part in relatively small-scale battles in Qalamoun in the Aleppo region, Lattakia and Al-Qamishli. That is the complete list. When it comes down to it, Baghdadi's men have *not* tried to confront the regime, and this has been true since the creation of the movement. Quite the reverse: they have concentrated their offensives on revolutionaries or the Kurds, with whom Islamic State competes for territory.

When I was in Raqqa in June 2013, a few weeks after the jihadi takeover of the city, I constantly puzzled over why the regime was dropping barrel bombs on civilian areas and causing widespread damage, while the jihadist leadership and the massive provincial governorate building in the city centre remained unscathed. (It was eventually bombed a year later, but by the US, not the regime.)

It is unsurprising that, in these circumstances, the groups conducting the Syrian uprising view Islamic State so negatively, or that Islamic State has an adversarial relationship with other jihadi movements such as Jabhat al-Nusra and Ahrar ash-Sham. The accusations of betrayal, even of collaboration with the regime, are some of the main charges made against Islamic State— even more so than its extremist stance or violent methods.

At the end of 2013, the moderate groups, tired of losing ground to Islamic State, lost patience when it took the border town of Azaz in the country's north-west. The control of borders is obviously a prime target for insurgents. It is through border crossings that contraband, weapons in particular, reaches Syria. They are also an important source of income, since the armed groups which control them impose taxes on goods in transit.[7]

In early January 2014, a coalition was formed (mainly between the Islamic Front and the Northern Storm Brigade), in order to dislodge Islamic State from its north-western strongholds. The jihadists were driven out of the cities of Atareb, between Aleppo and Hama, and al-Dana in the Jebel Zawiya. But this offensive was followed by a largely successful jihadist counter-attack, despite Islamic State having inferior numbers. The coalition also had the support of several countries, notably the United States, Turkey and several powerful Gulf states.

The researcher Romain Caillet of the Institut Français du Proche-Orient in Beirut has argued that Islamic State's victory was facilitated by its internal coherence when compared to less

---

[7] The economic aspects of the conflict are elaborated in chapter 3.

united insurgent groups in terms of ideology and command structure. Its 'unity ensures organisation and discipline in the field, which contrasts with those of the Free Syrian Army, whose soldiers are a mix of deserters and mafia gangs. It even contrasts with the cohesion of the Islamic Front, which is divided between moderate Islamists and Salafists. Even Jabhat al-Nusra does not possess such ideological coherence.'[8] In addition, a number of tribal alliances forged with Islamic State provided crucial support.

Despite some success in the north-west (such as the Idlib campaign and the seizure of Aleppo's north-west), this offensive was still overall a defeat. Islamic State conquered the countryside east of Aleppo, Raqqa and Deir ez-Zor. The conclusion to be drawn is unambiguous, however: moderate groups demonstrated their ability to take on Islamic State. They are the only ones to have done so in the field.

From summer 2014, as the West launched its air offensive against Islamic State, a new wave of cleansing took place, hurting the moderates in particular. On 9 September 2014, the Salafist group Ahrar ash-Sham, one of Islamic Front's mainstays, was decapitated. Around fifty members of the political and military leadership of 'The free men of Syria' (as the group's name translates) were killed in an explosion at an underground location near Idlib. Whether this was the work of Islamic State or the regime remains an open question.

Through October and into November, the other groups supported by the West suffered a series of defeats in the provinces of Idlib and Aleppo and in the Jebel Zawiya. The Revolutionary Front—a remnant of the Free Syrian Army—

---

[8] Romain Caillet, 'Echec de l'offensive de l'Armée syrienne libre contre l'Etat Islamique en Irak et au Levant', Orient XXI.info, 4 February 2014.

and the secular Hazem movement, were both driven out of their north-western strongholds. They were expelled by Jabhat al-Nusra, which then sought strategic control over the region. That jihadi group, an al-Qaida franchise, nevertheless enjoys real popularity in Sunni areas. This is the result of its genuine and effective fight against the regime. In the parts of Syria it controls, the population appreciates the fact that it plunders resources less than other armed groups, including the regime's militias. Sunnis also tend to consider Jabhat al-Nusra to be effective in protecting them against the regime's abuses.

Eventually, Abu Mohammad al-Julani sought recognition in the summer of 2014 and asked the United Nations to remove his group from the list of terrorist organisations. The group offered to withdraw from al-Qaida in exchange for this, but this did not seem to catch the attention of the great powers.

Yet in the West, the temptation to return to talks with the regime in the name of fighting terror is a recurrent phenomenon. The French daily *Le Monde* detailed how, at the end of March 2014, 'the French secret services wanted to re-establish communications with Damascus.'[9] This was in fact an initiative from the DGSI (*Direction générale de la sécurité intérieure*, the domestic intelligence), a decision taken, it seems, without coordination with either the Elysée Palace or the Foreign Ministry. It was a rash initiative also watched with great concern by the 'cousins' of the DGSE (*Direction générale de la sécurité extérieure*, the foreign intelligence). The aim was to re-launch technical police cooperation with the Syrian *Mukhabarat* to identify French jihadists on Syrian soil, out of a concern that they would return home to commit terrorist attacks.

[9] Jacques Follorou, 'Comment les services français ont voulu renouer avec Damas', *Le Monde*, 6 October 2014.

According to *Le Monde*, the Syrian intelligence services were flattered by this renewed offer of contact, but had a condition: the reopening of the French embassy in Damascus, closed since 6 March 2012, when France ceased to recognise the legitimacy of Bashar al-Assad.

Journalist Jacques Follorou writes in this article that 'though the DGSI may have significant technical and human resources to monitor candidates for the Syrian jihad on French soil and their communications, a precious link is missing: the jihadists' activities and movements inside Syria. The abrupt break in contacts between Paris and Damascus has diminished the source of information and, for two and a half years, has deprived the DGSI of data considered important.'

One of the main characters (and possibly also the instigator) of this attempt at rapprochement is Bernard Squarcini, former director of the DGSI's predecessor, the DCRI. Squarcini is a prominent figure in international policing and has maintained security networks in Damascus, which had been particularly active when Iraqi jihadist movements were at their peak. To this day, he is still very much influenced by the Syrian regime's version of events.

Apart from the fact that it would be immoral for the French police to collaborate with the Syrian intelligence services, who have been responsible for mass crimes since the revolution began, it would also be totally counter-productive. Bashar al-Assad is the worst possible partner to fight Islamic State. His intelligence services clearly lack information on the jihadists flooding into Syria. As these individuals enter the country secretly, it is impossible to cross-check visa registers or information from border police. Even their electronic surveillance of telephone calls and emails is very limited.

In Syria's 'liberated' areas, people do not depend on Syrian networks, which have either been cut off by the regime or largely destroyed by fighting. They communicate almost exclusively via Internet access relayed by satellite, to which the Syrian *mukhabarat* have little access and certainly much less than the secret services of powerful Western states. Only Syrian government agents who have infiltrated Islamic State's apparatus could be of any use. Their input, however, would remain marginal. It's probably possible to learn much more about European jihadists by carefully studying the texts and documents they post on social networks than by setting up a dangerous infiltration mission.

Asking the Syrian regime to help in the fight against Islamic State would not provide us with anything useful and would in fact create many problems, as the Islamic specialist Thomas Pierret explains:

> In all cases, the strictly military advantages of alliance with Assad are insignificant compared to the political drawbacks. Backing Assad and abandoning the rebels is equivalent to making Islamic State the regime's sole credible opponent, and therefore means throwing a large proportion of Sunnis, even the moderate ones, into its arms. This is exactly what happened in Iraq in recent years, with the difference that in Iraq Sunnis make up only 20 to 25 per cent of the population. To imagine that Assad can conclude a lasting alliance with credible Sunni forces to combat Islamic State is an aberration: first, because the regime's ability to be politically inclusive is close to nil, and second because, unlike in the case of the Iraqi government, there is not enough oil revenue to buy the loyalty of Sunni fighters.

So we must be wary of Bashar al-Assad's promises to 'help us' fight Islamic State and remember that he has no interest in the disappearance of the movement, which would mean the demise of a very useful bogeyman. As Emma Sky, a British adviser to the US military in Iraq, has explained: 'corrupt regimes and terrorists keep each other in business... It's a symbiotic relationship.'[10] The survival of Islamic State, which Assad has helped create, allows him to lump together this movement with secular demonstrators and regime opponents in order to blanket the entire dissident population of Syria with ruthless repression. Unlike the West, Assad knows who his real enemy is: a secular, non-sectarian opposition with political solutions for a new society free of Syria's Ba'ath dictatorship, a society whose rebirth and fledgling institutions he is trying to eliminate with barrel bombs filled with dynamite and chlorine gas. The regime has clearly revealed its strategy during the chemical weapons deal: to procrastinate. To play for time and manoeuvre. In the end, the regime's actions constantly betray its lies.

[10] Quoted in Michael Weiss and Hassan Hassan's book published in late 2014, *Isis: Inside the army of terror*, Regan Arts.

# 3

# Money Talks

*The revolution's economic and social roots shouldn't be forgotten. The regime and armed groups are fighting for control of revenue and resources.*

Syria has been a state inspired by a socialist vision since the coup of 1963, which brought the Ba'ath party to power. Its economic doctrine, however, has changed over time.

'For two decades from the early 1960s, Syrian socialist policies worked quite well. Schools, refineries and dams got built,' says Jihad Yazigi, an economist who runs several publications which specialise in Syria, among them the very useful syria-report.com. 'The regime was long able to keep the socialist ideal afloat and invest in development. The discovery of oil in the early 1980s began to derail this process. It is the curse of oil that its promise of quick wealth instantly provokes greed. Thereafter, high-ranking officers expected extra rewards for their loyalty to the president. At the same time, investment in development plummeted. "What's the use of continuing to invest?" leaders thought. They reckoned that oil would pay for everything. Reforms and liberalisation came to a halt as along with investments.'

Crisis hit in the 1990s. Oil revenues fell under the effects of declining production and the oil counter-shock, during a period when the population continued to grow. When he came to power in July 2000, Bashar al-Assad found himself in a corner and had to relaunch economic incentives, liberalise the economy and restart privatisation. This economic policy benefited a new elite and brought a new era of nepotism: prominent figures included Samer Douba, son of Ali, the old director of military intelligence; Rami Makhlouf, son of Mohammed, a businessman who has fled to Moscow, where he is trying to protect his fortune from economic sanctions; and Firas Tlass, the son of the ex-Defence Minister Mustafa, who has since joined the opposition.

Ayman Abdel-Nour, the opposition journalist and old university friend of Bashar al-Assad, is unforgiving when he describes the young president's methods: 'The entire economic system was conceived to serve the oligarchy. Hafez al-Assad used to give crumbs to Sunnis from Damascus and Aleppo in return for a bit of stability. But Bashar refused to budge an inch. He rearranged the whole system so that everything accrued to his family. For instance, he only reformed the banking system when family structures were in place to absorb it. His clan wanted to control all of Syria. He treats the entire country like his own house.'

The 'House of Assad' quickly became 'Assad, Inc.' It met in the winter of 2005, shortly after the Ba'ath party's tenth congress, amid the colonnades of a luxury hotel in the ancient Roman city of Palmyra in the eastern desert. In this luxurious setting, the regime's favoured businessmen agreed to divide up the country's entire wealth. The result of this 'Yalta of privatisations' was the creation of two holding companies, the Cham group, run by Rami Makhlouf, the president's cousin, and the Souria group. From then on, these groups split the country between them, tapping its wealth through participation in the government and taking public contracts. The architect of this reorganisation of the economy was not himself an economist. It was not even Abdullah Dardari, who was close to Bashar, who had been educated in Europe, spoke English and French fluently and had been appointed Vice President in charge of economic policy after being the representative in Damascus for the United Nations Program for Development (UNDP). Bashar did not even bother to put forward his useful front men, who were multi-lingual, well-presented and telegenic. Much more prosaically, it was General Bahjat Suleyman, who had left the internal branch of General Intelligence in June of the same year, who took charge of this 'reform'. Since the economy was a matter of national security, security agencies had to control resources. The subsequent years of Assad's rule until the start of the revolution were like one vast con game. On the one hand, the regime was notionally carrying out reforms and privatisations. Abdullah Dardari was in charge of putting a positive spin on the situation for the media, diplomats and expert panels. But behind the scenes the dice were loaded. Competition was impossible. The oligarchs close to power, who were members of 'the Family' or the security apparatus, had already divided the spoils. Corruption and sharp practice became the only games in town.

As Jihad Yazigi explains: 'In Syria, there have been no privatisations in the sense of sale of public assets, as happens in the West. There was just an opening-up of certain industries. The textbook example was the mobile phone market. There were two licences involved, and both clearly highly profitable, yet their allocation did not give rise to a genuine public tender. In the end, one licence went to Makhlouf and the other to Mikati [a pro-Syrian Lebanese tycoon who became Lebanon's Prime Minister after Saad Hariri].'

One businessman who paid a high price for his fight against cronyism is Riad Seif, who held the Adidas franchise in Syria and had been an independent MP since 1994. 'Since being elected, I have always been committed to fighting corruption. And this has had a high price. In 1996, they took my son and murdered him. In 1999, they orchestrated my bankruptcy.'

In 2001, Seif published a report proving that the mobile telephone licences had been awarded without any real competition and the contracts turned these markets into cash cows for whoever was awarded them. Because of his alleged political activity and hosting a discussion group in his home, the regime sentenced Seif to five years in prison. When he was released, he took the lead of the Damascus Declaration, an appeal for political pluralism. This led to his being arrested again at the end of 2007 and a further two-and-half years' incarceration. 'This regime is incapable of reforming itself,' is his bitter conclusion. 'In fact, it is even more a family oligarchy than a dictatorship. Bashar is convinced that Syria is his private property. And since the revolution began, he has shown that he would rather destroy Syria than lose it.'

Ayman Abdel-Nour told me: 'At the top level, Bashar al-Assad and Rami Makhlouf decide everything. Lower down, businessmen have to seek the protection of bigwigs in the intelligence services.' Jihad Yazigi refers to 'the patronage system of the secret services. If you open a hotel, you have to pay a *Mukhabarat* officer, or he will tip off a friend in the Tourism Ministry, who will produce a report saying you sell rotten food. They will shut your hotel down until you pay up.'

During this economic 'liberalisation' under the regime's tight control, economic elites focused their attention on the cities and ignored the countryside. Syrian agriculture suffered several consecutive years of drought, which led to disastrous harvests. Syrian peasants were marginalised and impoverished, and became the regime's first opponents. For long-term observers of the country, it was no surprise that the revolution began in Deraa, even though this southern town had been a Ba'ath party stronghold. The revolution is rooted in issues that are largely economic. The geography of the uprising is very telling and reveals motivations that go well beyond simple sectarian divides, the motive frequently put forward. The revolution revealed essentially economic and social fault lines, rather than a conflict between Sunnis and Shias as is generally supposed. The countryside rebelled first. By contrast, the Aleppo souk, though almost exclusively Sunni, long remained favourable to the regime.

The Lebanese political scientist Ziad Majed uses a Marxist-inspired framework to explain the revolution's origins. 'There is a class dimension to the Syrian revolution. Apart from students, intellectuals and activists, who played an important part in the early months, this revolution is mainly about the poor country folk, simple peasants for whom some of the new Syrian middle class have little sympathy. The new rich prefer to identify with the regime's "westernised" appearance, and the regime in addition protects its "deals", interests and businesses. There is also a strong element of social racism. People only want to see others who look "like us". People shut themselves off in a kind of bubble, and despise workers, vegetable sellers, cleaning ladies and all those who support them.' In fact, the revolt of Syrians had, at least at the start, a 'Communard' aspect: it was romantic, collectivist and libertarian. It is not very surprising that it soon came into conflict with various brands of conservatism.

When the revolution began, the people came up with their own solutions to fill the vacuum left by the state's failures. Syrian journalist Hala Kodmani describes how 'a spontaneous but very well organised movement sprang up as soon as there were free zones: the city's prominent citizens came together and created local councils. The people organised food supplies, schooling, hospitals and courts. This experiment failed for two reasons: first of all, the bombings by the regime, which particularly targeted civilians—especially schools and hospitals—and, secondly, because of the Islamic fundamentalists.' The rebellion, however, triggered competition for control of resources. The state soon had difficulty paying for the various militias and informal militiamen called *shabihha* it used to carry out repression (often ex-criminals in charge of the intelligence services' dirty work). The regime's henchmen were therefore authorised to 'live off the land'. When subduing a neighbourhood or retaking a village from the revolutionaries, they would not only attack the locals, but also loot and plunder. This was even shown live on television.

The day after the fall of the town of Al-Qusayr, on 5 June 2013, the BBC's special correspondent Lyse Doucet got permission from the authorities to visit this city recently 'retaken from the terrorists'. The regime was so pleased with its success, a real turning point in the revolution, that it granted access to an international TV channel to maximise publicity for its victory. The television crew had satellite technology, which meant Doucet could broadcast live from the streets and describe what she saw. Of course, the regime had planted a few residents to express their joy at the army's return. However, what was noticeable was the number of armed men, dressed in scruffy, unmatched fatigues, some with the yellow insignia of Hezbollah, laughing as they carried off everything they could load onto their motorbikes: furniture, televisions, computers, household appliances.

Later a market opened in Homs nicknamed *souq as-sunna* (the Sunnis' market), because its purpose was to sell the goods looted from this community. The political scientist Hamit Bozarslan explains that 'in Syria, we are witnessing an insane disintegration of the state, to the point that it is turning into a militia. According to Max Weber, the state is a mafia that has been successful. A "Westphalian" state, which has sovereignty over a territory, has the right to go to war to protect its society. However, in the present case, we are watching a mafia state destroying its own society to live off its very destruction.'[1]

Nevertheless, the regime does not have a monopoly on theft and looting. The descent into civil war led various *katiba* (brigade) leaders to begin behaving like unscrupulous warlords. Yassin al-Haj Saleh describes how 'armed groups have stripped the civilian population. You need them for everything—even just to eat. They want power. They want to control people. Among them are groups that are more open-minded, but their resources are more limited and they are weaker than the radical groups.' Armed gangs and militias have become major economic players. Wherever they have become established, they have replaced a failing state by providing basic services to the population, but also, and above all, by exploiting resources: factories, state farms, large bakeries, hydroelectric dams . . . Border controls and the access they give to 'custom duties' are particularly lucrative.

Jihad Yazigi told me:

> The control of border crossings and road checkpoints is one
> of the most important sources of income for rebel brigades.

[1] Lecture given on 30 November 2014.

There are some 34 checkpoints, for instance, along the 45 km between Aleppo and the Turkish border, i.e. one every 1.3 km. In Aleppo itself, the checkpoint in the Bustan al-Qasr district, which divides rebel areas from those held by the regime, was the focus of tough fighting between several groups, because controlling it made possible the collection of taxes on all the goods passing through. In practice, many rebel brigades are now more focused on developing their money-making activities than fighting the regime. For these people, as well as for many other individuals and groups on both sides of the conflict, war is a source of wealth and the prospect of its end would mean financial losses.

The country's main resource remains fossil fuels, however. It is therefore worth noting that although both the regime and Islamic State claim to be trying to free the people from the tyranny of each other, their main battleground is rarely around urban centres. The most fiercely contested territory is desert, which is rich in hydrocarbons. Fighting has mainly been aimed at conquering oilfields, refineries and pipelines. Syria has two oil-producing regions. The first lies between Deir ez-Zor and the Iraqi border. This was once a rich asset for Shell and Total, with a production of around 400,000 barrels a day in the 1980s, though nowadays it is reduced to barely 100,000. The second region is in the far north-east, between the cities of Al-Qamishli and Hassake, in an area where the regime has largely relinquished control to the PYD (Democratic Union Party) Peshmerga, the Syrian offshoot of the PKK (Kurdistan Workers' Party). This region's economy was still growing strongly when the revolution broke out, producing an average of 250,000 barrels a day. Around Deir ez-Zor, armed groups compete with one another to gain control of a share of the production from these oilfields, leading to violent fighting between rebel factions.

From a different viewpoint, the conflict is also being perpetuated because the different parties continue to receive funds from foreign sponsors. The regime no longer generates revenue in the normal way. Syria's middle and upper classes, dissatisfied with public services, have stopped paying their taxes. Oil exports have declined considerably. A strange triangular trade has developed as a result. Iran has become the chief provider of Damascus's hard currency and is directly paying for the weapon deliveries supplied by Moscow. Support for the rebels meanwhile comes mainly from the Gulf, from Diaspora businessmen and, to a lesser extent, from Turkey and the West. As far as I know, there is no study of the resources of all the insurgent groups (both revolutionaries and jihadists), but it is obvious that the rule 'who pays the piper calls the tune' applies. This rule has played its part in the radicalisation of the conflict since, when the revolution became an armed struggle, competition developed among *katibas* for financial backing from the Gulf. The different armed groups' media operations filmed their activities to attract sponsors. They soon realised that, the more their footage bore a thick Islamic veneer, the greater their success with donors, who viewed their donations as *zakat*, the Islamic tax which is one of Islam's five pillars. These donations have declined, however, because of measures against the funding of terrorism.

Islamic State has established the most efficient economy of all the insurgent groups; such was its success at financing itself that the Obama administration called it 'the best financed terrorist organisation in the world'. The illicit trade in oil from the fields it controls in Iraq and Syria brings in an estimated $1 million a day. Though this seems considerable, it is just a small fraction of an annual budget, which the United States estimates at two billion dollars. The intelligence services have difficulty identifying the intermediaries who buy this 'dirty' oil, which is sold clandestinely part-refined or unrefined. A network of dubious financiers launders the revenue from the sale through a series of frontmen. Among Islamic State's other sources of income have been the robbery of the Mosul Central Bank, from which they may have made as much as $480 million (a figure contested by several Iraqi officials), and money from trafficking antiquities.[2] Works of art from archaeological sites, museums or churches are sold to traffickers, particularly in Turkey (rumours abound: the trafficking of antiquities by Islamic State is so poorly documented that many people instead focus on the destruction of antiquities). Islamic State also controls several customs points at each of its 'borders' and extorts taxes of several hundred dollars per lorry. The Undersecretary of State to the American Treasury, David Cohen, has condemned the payment of 'at least twenty million US dollars in ransoms' paid over time to Islamic State for the release of hostages. This figure is of course impossible to verify and denied by all countries concerned.

The irony of it all is that Islamic State and the Syrian government are happy to do business together when it suits them. In January 2014, Ruth Sherlock, the *Daily Telegraph*'s Middle East correspondent, revealed the murky secrets of complex oil-trafficking between these two 'enemies'.[3] She

---

[2] The figure of €313 million is provided by Pierre-Jean Luizard, a scholar specialising in the modern history of Iraq, in his book *Le piège Daech: l'Etat islamique ou le retour de l'histoire*, La Découverte, Paris 2005.

[3] When I was in Raqqa in June 2013, several witnesses spoke of such agreements, both in this province and in Deir ez-Zor.

collected the testimonies of Western intelligence agencies, Syrian insurgents and al-Qaida defectors, and revealed what many Syrians had suspected. Crude oil extracted in government-controlled areas was being transported via pipelines to areas held by Islamic State and vice versa. This was proof enough of at least a tacit agreement between the two parties. Sherlock shone a light on the mendacity of these two supposed enemies: 'Assad's vow to strike terrorism with an iron fist is nothing more than bare-faced hypocrisy,' a Western intelligence agent told her. 'At the same time as peddling a triumphant narrative about the fight against terrorism, his regime has made deals to serve its own interests and ensure its survival.'

The first indications of these deals between the regime and the jihadists date from spring 2013, when Jabhat al-Nusra took control of some of the country's richest oilfields, in the eastern province of Deir ez-Zor. In January 2014 Sherlock reported that 'the regime is paying al-Nusra to protect oil and gas pipelines under al-Nusra's control in the north and east of the country, and is also allowing the transport of oil to regime-held areas.' The Homs and Banias refineries, in particular, never stopped being supplied with crude oil, despite the regime losing most of its oilfields. Many of the installations seized by Jabhat al-Nusra are now under Islamic State's control and there is nothing to suggest that these agreements with the regime have ended since.

On the Iraqi side of the border, Islamic State has seized oilfields around Mosul, and also on the edge of the Kurdish autonomous region. It fought the Iraqi army for control of the Baiji refinery, one of the most important oil facilities in the country.

Finally, and this is not the least of the inconsistencies, air strikes by the US have increased the suffering of civilians. In a well-sourced blog post[4], Jihad Yazigi has detailed the financial impact of this military campaign on Syrian players. The main targets of the bombings were, from the outset, the refineries under Islamic State control. The aim was to put an end to oil as a source of funding. Yazigi notes that 'while it is likely that Islamic State's finances will suffer from the destruction of refineries, it is not certain that the impact is as significant as Washington hopes. By contrast with refineries, most oilfields have not been hit and the Islamist organisation always has the means to sell oil as crude.' He notes that Islamic State has many other sources of revenue, notably in the form of taxes and duties levied in the areas it controls.

Jihad Yazigi mentions that the people, on the other hand, have had difficulty finding fuel. These shortages become particularly critical in winter, when the vast majority of the population heat their homes with diesel-burning stoves. This oil shortage has had an inflationary effect and caused a chain reaction; the price of basic products, especially agricultural ones, has increased due to transport costs, and the electricity supply, which, because the grid has been seriously damaged by war, largely depends on diesel generators, has declined still further. A few days after the first air strikes, the regime increased the price of diesel first by 33 per cent then by 17 per cent, with timing that might also betray the existence of movements of oil extracted in Islamic State-held areas and consumed in government-controlled parts of Syria.

The terrible irony of these air strikes is that people suffer more in the areas no longer under government control, whether they are held by the Free Syrian Army, Islamic State or another

---

[4] http://jihadyazigi.com/2014/11/06/lourd-impact-socio-economique-des-frappes-aeriennes-contre-lei-en-syrie/

rebel group. The regime is able to maintain the population's standard of living through substantial financial support from Iran and Russia. Quite the opposite occurs in areas freed from its yoke, with the partial exception of Kurdish regions.

Instability has destroyed the production economy, and created structures based on day-to-day survival and predation. All this has happened—inevitably—at the Syrian people's expense.

# 4

# A Self-fulfilling Prophecy

*The radicalisation of the Syrian revolution is the natural result of our inaction.*

To the people who approach me in restaurants or at the end of lectures and say with a rueful look: 'It's true that what's happening in Syria is a never-ending tragedy, but it's all so complicated . . .' and then go off with a sigh of despair, I usually respond with a story from the school playground.

It is the story of a schoolboy who, at each break, gets beaten up by another child. The pupil dutifully goes to the teacher to complain. She immediately says, 'Oh, you poor boy, what's happening to you is wrong.' She scolds the bully, saying, 'You're bad, stop at once or I'll punish you . . .' Except that each day, at each break, our child continues to get pummelled. The teacher, the headmaster and the supervisors of course reprimand the bully, but do nothing to stop him.

This goes on for some five years. That's how long the pupil has been getting beaten up. So he decides to join a gang to protect himself. A real gang of properly nasty characters. So everyone on the school staff jumps on him to criticise him. And the bully who used to beat him up now goes to see the teacher and brags, 'You see, I told you that boy was a violent thug!'

When I was a journalist in the Middle East, I often noticed that prophecies in this part of the world are self-fulfilling. It is often enough just to cry wolf to create a wolf. Violence produces violence, just as despair breeds radicalisation, and hate feeds hate.

From the time of my first report from Syria after the revolution broke out in September 2011, I worried that the nascent movement of popular dissent held the potential for violence. Yet at the time, it was not a war. There was no armed conflict. But descent into the worst type of violence already seemed unstoppable, as I wrote in the French weekly, *Le Point*:

This revolution has created chasms between communities that will be difficult to bridge. The regime is firmly holding onto its strongholds, the cities of Aleppo and Tartous, as well as a substantial part of Damascus. It can count on the unfaltering loyalty of the Alawis, most Christians and much of the business community. But it has alienated the Sunni majority, probably forever. Confronting the regime are the revolutionaries, who seem unable to recruit followers beyond their traditional territory: the poorest people, often from the countryside, and the few industrial cities of central Syria. In every case, allegiance to either Assad's regime or the revolution depends largely on people's religious community, to the extent that it can be plotted on a map. One village supports this side, while a second supports another. In cities, you can walk from a rebel neighbourhood into a loyalist one. Except that both rebel and regime-controlled areas are interwoven nationwide. The opposition is not able to create a consistent, contiguous and coherent base. On both sides, many have reached a point of no return. Most revolutionaries know they are being pursued by the regime, which will show no mercy. In addition, the henchmen who have carried out the repression of recent months have little chance of surviving regime collapse. For both sides, it's victory or death.[1]

The radicalisation of the revolution has proceeded in tandem with the hardening of Bashar al-Assad's personality; this is a man who allegedly chose ophthalmology when entering medical school because he could not stand the sight of blood. Between his university days—the period when Ayman Abdel-Nour socialised with him—and his rise to power, the somewhat inconspicuous nature of Hafez's heir was progressively replaced by the implacable harshness of the new president. The memories of his old friend, who stayed in touch with him till he came to power, have a certain piquancy:

Bashar al-Assad has had not one life, but three. The first Bashar lasted until the death of his brother Bassel [who would have been his father's heir]. He was a very normal guy. He was shy. He would hide his smile, because he didn't like his mouth, so he would always conceal his face when he laughed. He was always happy to do you a favour. The second Bashar is the one who came back from London to follow a military-training course. As he started out as a doctor, he lacked the respect of the army, in other words the status of a fighter. This is why he was taken out of the army health service and incorporated into the college of cavalry, because tanks are more manly. He started building up muscle. And his voice, which used to be reedy, got firmer. The third Bashar is the one who came to power. About a year and a half after he became president, he started behaving like he was God. That's when I stopped seeing him.

[1] 'A Homs, au cœur de la Syrie rebelle', *Le Point*, 6 October 2011.

In April 2013, when I was reporting from Jebel Zawiya, I began to realise that radicalisation was an unstoppable process. It automatically went hand in hand with criticism of Western inaction. 'If you do nothing to help us, we will all be al-Qaida!' How many times have I heard this sentence, uttered as a threat of last resort. I had gone to make a broadcast on Kafranbel for the TV channel *Arte*. Kafranbel was a town perched in the hills that had become famous on social networks for the humorous messages its inhabitants sent to the world. Raed Fares, a 'repentant Ba'athist', ran the revolutionaries' media centre with great imagination, while Ahmed, a former dental-prosthetics technician, became one of the most famous cartoonists of the Syrian uprising. In Kafranbel, people sang and danced and still had the strength to laugh. Whole families went to demonstrations together. While the war raged, and bombs and shells dropped almost daily, revolution was still in an age of innocence.

When I arrived, I discovered that Jabhat al-Nusra was achieving victories in the region. I was surprised to see that this was happening without too much friction with other rebel factions. When it was founded in spring 2012, when the Homsi neighbourhood of Baba Amr was under siege from the Syrian army, Jabhat al-Nusra initially enjoyed the esteem of its countrymen. Fairly well organised, honest, effective in battle, with a limited use of suicide attacks (jihadists only ever call them 'martyrdom operations'), its members were, in the eyes of Syrians, an efficient bulwark against the regime, even though most did not share their extremely conservative political, religious and social views. Jabhat al-Nusra was keen to show itself worthy of its name: 'Front of the support' in Arabic, or to give it its full name, 'Front of the Support to the Syrian population of the mujahadin of the Sham Region in the Jihad

Arena. It did not balk at taking on the army and intervening when the latter attacked. It was always careful to distinguish between civilian and military targets.

Yet during my time in Kafranbel, what one of the Free Syrian Army commanders told me was unambiguous:

> If the Syrian people are left like this, they will be taken over by genuine jihadi tendencies. People will gravitate to the Islamist movements. We are all moderate Muslims, but if we are abandoned in the battlefield, we will turn towards extremism. It will be an honour for us! Five or six hundred people are dying every day. They want us to remain spectators, but we will not. The world will pay the price, because the Syrian people will not obey the Security Council or the UN, not human rights organisations or anybody else. Since we are left to ourselves, we have the right to respond by ourselves, by whatever means we see fit. The Syrians are one people, the armed and the unarmed, employees and labourers. We have a united network, standing up to the regime. The people will turn towards what they think is best for them. We are all united on the ground: the Syrian people, the Free Syrian Army, Jabhat al-Nusra. This is because Jabhat al-Nusra, which the West calls terrorists—all these definitions suit Westerners, but not us—is part of Syria's social fabric. It can't be separated from the people. These are political games and the Syrian people know it. Their aim is the collapse of the Syrian people itself. Not the collapse of Bashar al-Assad's regime. The silence of the whole world has an aim: the collapse of the Syrian people.

The success of Islamist groups stems from several factors: their apparent military effectiveness, their image of integrity (which often makes them popular among the people), but also from the way they raise money, which is an incitement to step up the religious rhetoric. Political Scientist Ziad Majed has noted that 'the main factor leading to radicalisation is that the better-equipped groups attract the most new recruits. This has enabled the growth of jihadist groups, since they were the ones who had the best backers.'

Jabhat al-Nusra's popularity confused things. Yet despite its allegiance to al-Qaida, the West did not find it sufficiently worrying to stop their assistance to the Syrian revolution. So the regime continued to push the radicalisation of the conflict, contributing both to Jabhat al-Nusra's increasing sectarianism, and the creation of Islamic State. This is why Jabhat al-Nusra, which had previously been selective in its choice of targets, changed tack in summer 2013, after the chemical attack on the Ghouta. The movement decided to be more sectarian by increasingly attacking 'Alawi targets'.

Simultaneously, Jabhat al-Nusra's relationship with revolutionary groups deteriorated, while it was itself being swallowed up by Islamic State. General Salim Idriss, who had until then been receiving support from abroad in the form of weapons and fighters, subsequently began to describe Islamic State jihadis as 'criminals' and 'regime agents'. The relationship between the three main jihadi movements became more complicated. Islamic State mobilised violence and sectarianism in the name of purity of the *Sunna*. It began exploiting frustrations, and developed a brand of demagoguery that targeted its victims. It also discovered that a radicalised jihad is very effective in attracting foreign recruits, radicals who show little respect for local customs, and even less for local people.

Ahrar ash-Sham, a 'constitutionalist' jihadi movement, has combined armed struggle in Islam's name with democratic institutions. It declared a wish to participate in elections following the regime's downfall, and soon found itself fighting Islamic State in several regions, particularly Raqqa. Jabhat al-Nusra hesitated between these two groups, sometimes making temporary pragmatic alliances, sometimes joining forces with other groups, while fighting them elsewhere. Yassin al-Haj Saleh, a secular intellectual, explains, 'the main difference between Jabhat al-Nusra and Islamic State is that the members of Jabhat are mainly Syrians and its agenda is essentially Syrian. By contrast, Islamic State has an international agenda and has incorporated many *muhajrin* ('émigrés'—as foreign fighters who join jihadist movements are called). But their ideology is very similar.'

One of Jabhat al-Nusra's priorities is to avoid *fitna*, an internecine struggle between Muslims.

Yassin al-Haj Saleh worries about how the conflict will develop: 'The longer the regime lasts, the more radicalisation and sectarianism there will be. There are more and more sectarian massacres. People have killed the inhabitants of neighbouring villages. And this benefits the fundamentalists most of all, and of course the regime.'

Ziad Majed believes that 'the difference between jihadi groups is not so much ideological, but derives from their make-up. Most members of Jabhat al-Nusra and Ahrar ash-Sham are Syrian. Most of Islamic State's recruits (certainly the early ones) are foreign. This dates back to the split between Jabhat al-Nusra and Islamic State: Julani kept most of the Syrians, while almost all of the foreigners joined Baghdadi. There has been a real war in Deir ez-Zor between Jabhat al-Nusra and Islamic State, which has cost thousands of lives. The problem is that instead of trying to find a way to divide these two groups and bring Jabhat al-Nusra back to the revolutionary fold, the current American intervention risks strengthening solidarity between jihadists. Negotiators must be found within both Jabhat al-Nusra and Ahrar ash-Sham, in order to bring them back to the revolution eventually.'

It seems obvious to everyone I've met in Syria since the revolution began that the country needs international assistance to finish off Assad's dictatorship. But it has taken a long time for Syrians to realise that this assistance will never come, and that realisation has been painful. There have been innumerable calls for help from revolutionary groups. In October 2011, a request for a no-fly zone. In December 2011, a request for a humanitarian buffer zone, in which displaced people could seek protection. In January 2012, there was a request for clear support for the Free Syrian Army. In March 2012, a request for an international military intervention to put an end to massacres. In August 2012, a request for anti-aircraft weaponry, and so on . . . It had long been clear that the Syrian regime's superior airpower gave it a decisive advantage, making the Free Syrian Army's sacrifices count for nothing. In June 2013, President Hollande of France was still pondering how weapons that could bring down the regime's fighter jets might be delivered.

Ziad Majed insists that 'the West, and particularly the US, has indirectly maintained the imbalance of forces. Weapon deliveries and limited political support have enabled the regime to maintain its firepower and its air force to bomb all over the country, despite its loss of legitimacy among the people.'

The most shameful inaction followed the chemical bombing of the Ghouta in August 2013, which resulted in 1,400 deaths. Initially the regime panicked. Observers in Damascus thought the upper echelons of the regime were preparing to flee, convinced that Western intervention was imminent. But on the contrary, the absence of reaction was finally taken as giving the regime carte blanche; it realised that the West would never do anything. Assad immediately intensified the brutality of his attacks, and insidiously reintroduced chlorine, his chemical weapon of choice. There was no reason to take the international community's sabre-rattling seriously when it was incapable of responding convincingly to its own 'red lines' being crossed.

Historian and publisher Farouk Mardam Bey, who was one of the Syrian revolution's earliest supporters, agrees that 'since the lack of any Western reaction to the chemical bombing of the Ghouta, regime bombing has doubled in ferocity and now targets the civilian population much more viciously to cause the maximum number of civilian casualties. We have seen the advance of the Syrian army on the ground, with militia support, while watching a media offensive intent on conveying the message: "it's either Daesh [Islamic State] or the regime." Media spotlights have changed sides. When foreign journalists went mainly to liberated areas, these areas ended up being abandoned by the press because of kidnappings precisely when the regime was opening its gates and welcoming an increasing number of Western media, to put its message across.'

Why did the West pull back? It would be too simplistic to cite our governments' cowardice. The arguments for non-intervention are well known: the fear that weapons will 'fall into the wrong hands' (a fear expressed well before the so-called dreaded 'wrong hands', those of the jihadists, appeared in Syria). The rebels have also been much criticised for their weakness and factionalism. But this is hardly surprising, given how many groups and states with vested interests have tried to dictate the agenda: the Gulf States who support the insurgents for Sunni supremacy, motivated by the phobia of a 'Shia Crescent'; the Turks, who have imperialist designs; Westerners demanding that the Free Syrian Army be a bulwark against Islamist terrorism; the US, which has its favourites; and the European powers, which have theirs; and the never-ending competition between the Saudis and the Qataris, both of whom finance their protégés. In such a situation, how could there be any hope that revolutionary *katibas*, additionally subjected to their own local political games, would unite and be effective as a national army as soon as they emerged from secrecy? Ziad Majed points out that 'Qatar and Saudi Arabia are not democratic states. They are not necessarily interested in the Syrian people's freedom. They want to weaken Iran and Russia, two other undemocratic states, which also protect the Syrian regime for geostrategic, but also strictly sectarian, reasons.' Farouk Mardam Bey adds, 'Competition between Saudi Arabia and Qatar has greatly contributed to the implosion of the opposition', not to mention the divergence of views among Western countries, which have not been able to articulate a single policy based on a common objective.

Criticism of Syria's revolutionaries in fact demonstrates our barefaced hypocrisy. President Obama has admitted that he has no strategy for the Syrian crisis. European diplomats hide behind Russia's veto at the Security Council, effectively paralysing the international community. Gérard Araud, French ambassador to the UN until the summer of 2014, is very familiar with the Syrian crisis: 'Russia has used its veto four times over Syria, something we've never seen before!' He concludes that 'this is clearly proof that the United Nations cannot resolve all conflicts. It only solves the conflicts that the great powers want to allow it to solve.'[2]

[2] Meeting with the press in Paris in September 2014.

Russia's opposition did ultimately come as a relief to the West and allowed its leaders to pass the buck for their inaction.

Several nations' militaries made intervention plans for Syria. However, in every case, fear prevailed. Too complicated. Too risky. Too many unknowns. A regime which was still too powerful. And, ultimately, too high a cost for intervening (including potential terrorist reprisals, like the ones Iran perpetrated in France in the 1980s) compared to the negligible political benefit. Western public opinion has come to terms with it: the Syrian people are the victims of fate and nothing can be done about it. France's lack of enthusiasm for showing solidarity with the Syrian revolution is a sad illustration of this. In comparison to all the challenges French society faces—the dogma of economic growth, unemployment, debt, deficits—Syria's dead count for almost nothing to the electorate. Yet diplomatic pressure can produce results. Farouk Mardam points out that 'the regime will not retreat, without a change in Russian and Iranian attitudes. Unfortunately it's unlikely that this attitude will change, even if the Russians do have some fear of Western intervention against Islamic State, which might instil more realism in the Kremlin's policies.'

Islamist groups have themselves tried as hard as possible to resist the trap of extremism. Frantz Glasman, a consultant on Syria, cites the 'Charter of revolutionary honour of fighting brigades', which was signed on 18 May 2014. [3] This charter 'affirms their participation in support of the revolutionary movement. [It] explicitly rejects all forms of totalitarian

[3] Frantz Glasman, 'Vie locale et concurrence de projets politiques dans les territoires sous contrôle de l'opposition, des djihadistes et des Kurdes en Syrie', Paris, October 2014.

Islamic governance. It stresses that the downfall of the regime must lead to justice, not revenge. It specifically treats Islamic State and its *Takfiri* practices as enemies to be combatted, to the same extent as the regime and its armed supporters. It calls for collaboration between all rebel forces and is open to cooperation with foreign countries. It is committed to preserving Syria's unity. It confirms that political and military decisions must remain in the hands of Syrians, which is an about-face on the question of "foreign" involvement in the country. Finally, it emphasises that the Syrian revolution aims at the establishment of the rule of law and freedom for all Syrians, of all religious communities and ethnic groups, and is committed, as regards these aims, to respect human rights.'

The prophecy has been self-fulfilling. In their misfortune, Syrians, universally abandoned, have increasingly, and understandably, looked to God. Faced with crimes on such a scale and continuous exposure to extreme violence, confronting fear, despair, ever-present death, how could anyone criticise their need to believe? The Christian Ayman Abdel-Nour has explained this movement towards Allah best: 'All Syrians who fight need God in order to die in his name. Syrians are religious people. Even the Christians, during the wars against Israel, shouted *Allahu akbar* when they attacked. This is the army's official war cry. It's cultural, not religious. I too spent my military service shouting *Allahu akbar*! I would not be willing to die under Lenin or Castro's banner . . . Most revolutionaries brandish the black banner, but that's because it's the only one available. There is no other, and even Christians die under it.'

In addition, since moderate groups were trapped in a vice, bearing the brunt of most of the regime and Islamic State's attacks, conditions were ripe for the radicalisation of the opposition. Ignace Leverrier, the pen name of a retired French diplomat previously posted in Damascus, summarises very persuasively in his blog the reasons why Islamic State has such success in recruiting. First he notes that Islamic State managed to recruit 6000 Syrians in August 2014 alone. This was a watershed in Islamic State's history, since these new recruits completely altered the composition of the movement's personnel, who had previously been mainly foreigners. This transformed it into an organisation with a Syrian majority. Leverrier lists the reasons for this:

The savagery of the regime's behaviour since the uprising began, and the crimes committed by sectarian militias cooperating with Assad against the Syrians since 2012.

The abandonment of the Syrian revolution by the West, and the general feeling among Syrians of being victims of a plot.

The order, planning, discipline and power of Islamic State compared to revolutionaries who lack the means to organise themselves.

The substantial wages the group pays its fighters, which the Free Syrian Army has never had the means to match.

The fascination exerted by Islamic State's power, and its propaganda success, which focuses on the heroism of commandos, who don't fear death.

The international community's hostility towards moderate Islamist factions and its reservations about the Islamic dimension of the Syrian revolution.

Islamic State's exploitation of sectarian instincts and the attraction of people to passionate religious sermons offering an alternative to the Umma's weakness and paralysis.

It is not surprising that finally—like the schoolboy I mentioned at the beginning of this chapter—the Syrian people, exhausted and deeply vulnerable after three years of savage repression—have sought refuge with the strongest group, the one with the biggest muscles and, however ugly it is, the one that seems best able to protect them. The Beirut-based scholar Romain Caillet describes the allegiance of Syrian tribes to Islamic State in the Jerablus and Raqqa regions: 'In Raqqa, some tribes who want stability and are convinced that Bashar's regime will never return, have turned to Islamic State, sometimes without any ideological consideration.'[4] He highlights the case of the Afadila, who went without any transition from the regime's camp to Islamic State's. This tribal survival instinct, divorced from any political stance, has at times led to unlikely U-turns. Other tribes have been pragmatic and dispersed their members among all the armed groups in the field. 'When fighting broke out in Raqqa between pro- and anti-Islamic State militias, most of the city's tribes with sons on both sides distanced them from the battlefield to avoid them killing each other, forcing the city's anti-Islamic State militias to appeal to Salafis from the Idlib and Aleppo Islamic Front, in order to support the revolutionary brigades of Raqqa allied to Jabhat al-Nusra.'

In Jerablus, Islamic State exploited local tribal enmities to retake the border town. The story sounds like a movie synopsis. On one side were the Jays tribe, who are secular and were loyal to the regime before joining the Free Syrian Army. On the other were the more conservative Tayy, whose members had thrown in their lot with Jabhat al-Nusra before joining Islamic State. The town was liberated in July 2012 when regime forces abandoned all their positions in the Syrian north to

---

[4] Romain Caillet, 'Echec de l'offensive de l'Armée syrienne libre contre l'Etat Islamique en Irak et au Levant', *op. cit.*

concentrate on the 'useful' regions of the country, after being faced with a particularly well-coordinated Ramadan offensive. The two competing tribes had equal claims to be in charge of Jerablus: the Jays had provided the uprising with one of its most distinguished officers, who died in combat. The Tayy had among their members one of the town's most popular imams, whose three brothers had died as martyrs. The murder of a foreign jihadist in town led to clashes between the two tribes. With Islamic State support, the Tayy won and, in the summer of 2013, brought this strategic border town under Islamic State control.

Romain Caillet concludes that 'in Jerablus as in Raqqa, and probably in other cities, many inhabitants willing to see the return of order and security in town have reconciled themselves as much as they can to the presence of Islamic State fighters.' He quotes a local: 'At the beginning, my parents were against Islamic State, but today they still prefer their authoritarian behaviour to the anarchy prevailing in places controlled by the FSA (Free Syrian Army). It is true that with the FSA we were free to do as we pleased, but with them the city was not secure and we could be kidnapped by gangs at any time.'

Given that, to date, Islamic State has played the tribal card skilfully, the same local knowledge will be required if we want local allies willing to fight Islamic State for the sake of their security as well as ours.

# 5

# Who's Killing Whom? And, More Importantly, How Many?

*The West is obsessed with the security risk the jihadists represent. Local people, however, are the jihadists' main casualties. And the worst terrorists are regime forces.*

Sometimes I get angry on camera. It happened once when Finnish public television's Paris correspondent asked me in an interview, 'Aren't you afraid of the jihadi threat? After all, there are more than a thousand French people involved in the jihad in Syria. Is this not a serious danger?'

I was too stunned to speak for a moment. Then I got annoyed.

At the time of writing, only one of these French jihadists has returned to Europe and is suspected of having committed a terrorist attack: Mehdi Nemmouche, who is accused of killing four people—including two Jews and a Muslim—in the Jewish Museum in Brussels. I am not for a moment denying the danger such people may pose to Europe's security—just putting it in perspective, indeed seeing it from the viewpoint of Iraqis and Syrians. In their eyes, who are these thousand French nationals? They are criminals, thugs, a product of our society's ills, whom we export and who vent their anger in their murderous rampages. Take Mehdi Nemmouche, arguably the embodiment of our nightmares come true: how many people did he kill during his year in Syria? Potentially far more than the four deaths he is accused of in Brussels. Will he ever be held to account for his Syrian victims? Does anyone care about them?

Before becoming obsessed by the security risk posed by these jihadists—the products of our societies—it would be good to put aside our self-centredness and think about what crimes our fellow citizens might have committed in Syria and Iraq. Many Westerners have called for suicide attacks. And how many murders? How many acts of torture? How can we be so sensitive to our own security when we deny others the right to live in safety? Extremism feeds on this kind of double standard.

When it comes to Islamic State, Western outrage is all the easier, since the organisation records its crimes. Media display of violence is both a form of cathartic revenge, and also a means of terrorising the enemy. Beheadings, crucifixions, summary executions are shown ad nauseam.

The political scientist François Burgat explained in an interview with RFI radio following the murder of American journalist Steven Sotloff that 'Islamic State does not in my view commit more violent acts—individual or collective—than the other parties to the conflict, particularly the Syrian regime. What Islamic State does is simply integrate them into its PR policy, while the Syrian regime denies its acts of violence and places responsibility on the enemy. Islamic State uses violence as an integral part of its communication. This is the communication policy of the weak. When you're in a dominant position, you don't have to try to scare the enemy.'

According to the London-based Syrian Observatory for Human Rights (SOHR), Islamic State executed nearly 1500 people during the five months following the establishment of its caliphate. Among them were 900 civilians, including 700 members of the Shaytat tribe, which had opposed Islamic State, but also approximately sixty rival jihadists belonging to Jabhat al-Nusra. SOHR has also counted 500 regime soldiers who were killed, either in combat or following capture (the killing of captives is a routine war crime in Syria's civil war).

My purpose here is not to diminish the scale of these crimes. Quite the opposite, as a victim myself of Islamic State, I feel I have some legitimacy in condemning its violence. However, for six murdered hostages, how many Syrians and Iraqis have been tortured or killed? The scale of this violence is overwhelming. Our self-preservation instinct probably prevents us from seeing it. Yet this violence must not be ignored. We should at least have the decency to try to understand the disgust of Syrians, who, even after more than 200,000 people have been killed, see that the West is only affected by the beheading of its hostages. These were my friends and I am bereaved. This is all the more reason for me to not to allow their deaths be exploited for unscrupulous ends.

Quite the opposite, there needs to be a sense of proportion and a focus on the scale of these crimes. This leads to an obvious conclusion: the regime is simultaneously the instigator of the violence and its main perpetrator. The Syrian Network for Human Rights (SNHR) was founded in May 2011 to precisely document the victims of repression. The revolution was then a joyful, peaceful affair. It was imaginative and good-natured. Demonstrations had a street party atmosphere. Rebels were almost having fun, thwarting arrest by the political police. But the crackdown got tougher, and it stopped being a game. Since the start of the revolt, SNHR has collated tens of thousands of reports of deaths, arrests, imprisonments, torture and sexual violence. Its methodology, as set out on its website,[1] is highly rigorous: its main limitation is not derived from the fact that cases may have been invented, but that many of them were not counted in calculations because they were not supported by sufficient evidence. This is why Fadel Abdul-Ghany, SNHR's president and founder, admits they have little information on regime or Islamic State losses, 'because we have no sources inside these groups. By contrast, the information we have on casualties we list is very complete, with their names, age, profession all mentioned . . . We have remotely trained people who work for us in all of the provinces. They are in constant contact with local committees. Some of these correspondents who work for us have more than 3,000 contacts on their Skype account. But we always check information and ask for evidence, ideally photographic.

The most credible assessments mention more than 200,000 people killed since the uprising began, but also quote a similar figure for the disappeared, political prisoners, hostages or others flung into pits. Many of these disappeared are probably already dead. It is likely that most detainees will never be seen again. In the end, it is probably reasonable to estimate that the Syrian conflict's total number of casualties will be at least double what has already been acknowledged. SNHR has only been able to list the names of 5,600 people killed under torture, while 'Caesar's' photographs show the bodies of 11,000 different people, murdered in just two detention centres in Damascus. In most cases, however, names are lacking. Or victims have not been recognised by relatives and are still counted among the disappeared.

In late September 2014, the network published a report on the conflict's total number of confirmed victims: Fadel

[1] http://sn4hr.org/blog/2014/09/22/169

Abdul-Ghany said that his network had 'discovered that the regime has killed 150 times more civilians than Islamic State'. 125,000 casualties caused by the regime, against fewer than 850 caused by Islamic State. This disparity should come with three important qualifications: first, the regime has been killing people since the revolution began, while Islamic State appeared on the stage only in April 2013. Second, SNHR has better access to regime victims than to those of the jihadists. Third, this is a tally of civilian casualties only; it is likely that Islamic State kills a higher proportion of soldiers, while the regime concentrates on the repression of civilians. But even if these three caveats alter the proportions, they do not contradict this conclusion: the Syrian security forces are by far the main killers and remain the fundamental threat to the Syrian people. This is how Syrians feel, and no political solution can be found unless it addresses this fear and their need for protection.

'People have a right to be protected and live in security,' human rights activist Fadel Abdul-Ghany told me. 'No one is protecting them, and the war and killings go on.' He pointed out the incoherence of Western rhetoric about protecting civilians which only attacks Islamic State and continues to ignore the regime's crimes. 'Focusing on Islamic State means turning your back on your responsibilities, but also the implementation of reforms and real measures. The regime has committed ethnic cleansing. If such violence occurred in any country, France for instance, and the world looked on and condemned without doing anything, of course part of the French population would become extremist and begin committing crimes in turn. I fear the emergence of groups even more extreme than Islamic State.'

The regime is well aware how obsessed we are with jihadists and knows exactly how to play on it. Is it accidental that every bloodbath organised by Islamic State is followed by redoubled violence by the army? The bombing of Aleppo's suburbs is never so severe as on the days when the videos of Islamic State hostages being decapitated are released. While the world was looking at the face of Peter Kassig, an aid worker who had converted to Islam and whose big mistake was being too trusting, a mass grave was discovered near Homs containing the corpses of 381 men, women and children from the Baba Amr neighbourhood—people executed by regime militias. But who talked about them? Media attention will be focused elsewhere as long as we are obsessed with the jihadist threat. And the regime will go on gassing, maiming, killing and torturing.

Since Hafez al-Assad's time, Syria has stood out as one of the seven countries where torture is used most frequently. Bassam al-Ahmad is a human rights activist at the NGO Violations Documentation Center in Syria (VDC), which has published several reports on the frequent use of violence against prisoners. He explains that '57,000 cases of imprisonment and 2,300 cases of disappearances have been documented. There are hundreds of detention centres in Damascus alone. There are four security service divisions in Syria, each with its own network of secret prisons. More than 90 per cent of prisoners we know about have been tortured.' Bassam al-Ahmad was himself held for three months in spring 2012. He admits he was lucky to have been subjected only to what he calls 'light torture'.

In November 2013, the VDC published a chilling report on torture in two specific detention centres in Damascus, both run by military intelligence.[2] The report noted that as the revolution entered its third year, the regime kept inventing new methods intended to break the bodies and wills of detainees. In the two centres studied by the NGO, thousands of people who died

[2] http://www.vdc-sy.info/index.php/en/reports/1384453708

under torture were summarily buried. The document highlights the case of a humanitarian activist called Mohammed Mustafa Darwish, who was arrested in the south of Damascus while he was giving aid to displaced people. Mustafa was taken to branch 215, nicknamed 'hell's branch'. He was locked up in a communal cell six metres by twenty, two levels below ground in what had previously been a shooting range. He was held with about 440 other detainees. This room was a cell where prisoners were 'prepared' by long sessions of collective flogging. At this stage, there was no interrogation, no charges, nor anybody to explain the reasons for his arrest. It was a holding zone: he was there for a week just to be 'prepared'. When he came out, he was nicknamed 'Abu Zreiq' ('the blue one') by co-detainees, because he was one enormous bruise. He was then taken to an interrogation room, completely naked but for a small cloth blindfold over his eyes. His interrogator, who introduced himself as a high-ranking officer, beat and insulted him. He then accused him of being in possession of 'terrorist material'. He was then given two days' respite before being brought back to the interrogation room. There they went through his personal details before the torture began again. A long catalogue of horrific treatment went on uninterrupted for four days, carried out by four agents working in shifts. During the remainder of his detention, Mohammed was mainly subjected to beatings, long periods of suspension, including three days left hanging from the ceiling by one foot, and various forms of suffocation, particularly with a plastic bag. He had to spend days with his own excrement, and was given almost no food. The guards had also set up 'bicycle torture': a bicycle cogwheel set in a wall, which lacerates the backs of detainees for long periods. At the end of his period of imprisonment, Mohammed admitted to all of the charges against him.

Another report from Bassam al-Ahmad's NGO deals with the regime's repeated use of chemical weapons[3], despite Syria's commitments under the chemical disarmament agreement, following the attack on the Ghouta in August 2013. In order to avoid provoking the international community too much, since this date the regime has mainly used chlorine, whose classification as a chemical weapon has been under debate. The use of chemical weapons in small quantities is still a daily occurrence, and is done in defiance of international law and Syria's commitments. Despite this, Bassam al-Ahmad refuses to split hairs. 'Of course, if you merely look at numbers, the regime is much more murderous. Yet as defenders of human rights, we look at actions. For us, any crime is a crime.'

Donatella Rovera is special advisor to Amnesty International on crisis response. In recent years she has visited Iraq and Syria several times to investigate human rights violations. She shares Ahmad's view. In all conflicts, she emphasises, crimes are committed by all parties. Even by 'moderates':

'The facts are always important. It is clear that the regime causes more deaths because it conducts aerial bombings, which kill entire families. But I've had long discussions with the opposition from the start of the revolution, about the militarisation of the conflict and the fact of accepting "blunders", as they call them. Even among moderates, violent and completely unacceptable practices soon occurred, such as torture and mass murders, like the Berri family's elimination when a sizeable part of Aleppo fell.'

Violence is widespread and murder is always unacceptable, but the number of victims should not be overlooked.

[3] http://www.vdc.info/index.php/en/reports/1400970048

# 6

# Syria and Iraq: Two Countries, One Destiny

*The Iraqi and Syrian crises are linked. Any policy that treats them separately is bound to fail.*

The birth of Islamic State could almost be pinpointed to February 2003, when Colin Powell was sent by George Bush to the United Nations Security Council to furnish the world with 'evidence' of Saddam Hussein's guilt, evidence that would justify the urgent need to topple him. Among Colin Powell's 'findings'—and there were some gems—was the 'missing link': the man who was the link between Osama bin Laden and Saddam Hussein. The person who, by means of the remarkable rhetorical elasticity of Bush's America, would enable Iraq to be linked to the 'global war on terror'.

This man was Abu Musab al-Zarqawi. Zarqawi's relationship with bin Laden was based more on conflict than complicity, but let's pass over the errors of fact. In his early days as a jihadist, Zarqawi had thrown in his lot with Gulbuddin Hekmatyar. Zarqawi had met Osama bin Laden in 1999, a meeting that, according to Michael Weiss and Hassan Hassan,[1] 'went quite

[1] Michael Weiss and Hassan Hassan 2014, *Isis—Inside the army of terror*, Regan Arts, p. 11

badly. Bin Laden suspected him and the cabals of Jordanians he had arrived with of being infiltrated by the GID [Jordanian intelligence]. Besides, the ex-con's many tattoos, which Zarqawi had amassed in his less pious days and then tried and failed to erase with hydrochloric acid in prison, also disturbed the puritanical Saudi. Moreover, it was Zarqawi's arrogance, his "rigid views" that offended bin Laden. Al-Zawahiri was present at the meeting and agreed that the Jordanian was not a prime candidate for membership of al-Qaeda.'

Let us also set aside the fact that Zarqawi had nothing to do with Saddam (since he was in hiding in the Sulaymaniyah area, an autonomous Kurdish province, then completely beyond Baghdad's authority). But, with the sole aim of personalising the war on terror, and making it more 'sellable' to public opinion by giving it a media face, Powell created a legend and transformed a second-rate jihadist, who was completely peripheral in Al-Qaida's world-organisation chart, into a very effective rival of Osama bin Laden. A rival powerful enough to create an organisation, Islamic State, which is probably Al-Qaida's main threat today.

To understand how the crises are intertwined, we have to go back to Iraq's history since the US invasion, in particular to US governance of the country and the history of resistance to the invasion. The occupation of Iraq got off to a very bad start for the United States. While other media were waxing lyrical about Iraq's armed forces, I drew attention to the exhaustion of the civilian population in my reports. Iraqi society had suffered greatly from two decades of war and sanctions, and was on the point of collapse.[2] Saddam knew this. In the last months

---

[2] This can be observed in the documentary *Tonnerre roulant sur Baghdad* ('Thunder driving over Baghdad', on the Arte channel, 2012), which I shot with Jean-Pierre Kreif.

of his rule, he had called on Muslims from all over the world to come and fight the invaders.

Jihadism did not exist in Iraq before the United States threatened the country. However, after 7 April 2003, I saw no trace of the Iraqi regime on the streets of Baghdad. The only fighters doing their best to prevent the Americans' entry by harassing tanks with RPGs, and playing hide-and-seek in deserted streets and in the reed beds by the Tigris, were jihadists—Palestinians, Yemenis and Egyptians as well as Syrians.

They welcomed me without any fear and let me accompany them in combat. On 8 April, I was surprised to see them shooting at both sides. A machine gun burst on Americans coming into town, another on pick-ups full of Iraqis. I then realised that the pick-ups were carrying Shias, who had started looting. These were the first sectarian fault lines. I later went to Firdos Square, where the famous statue of Saddam Hussein stood, a statue that dozens of Iraqis were trying to deface and topple, soon aided by US soldiers and their armoured crane. I was intrigued by what the crowd were shouting. I thought I heard the name 'Ali' and asked an Iraqi man to explain. 'We shall never forget Imam Ali!' he told me, referring to one of the most revered figures in the Shia tradition. I couldn't believe this, and asked him to repeat it. But I had heard correctly. While news reporters from around the world celebrated the euphoria of these Iraqis supposedly celebrating the end of dictatorship and the advent of a democracy, I was stunned. I began thinking of the disaster ahead. How could the situation avoid turning into a huge outburst of sectarian revenge?

Meanwhile in the United States, George Bush had been caught out in a live television interview. He admitted he did not know the difference between Sunnis and Shias, which was crass, but revealing. The sectarian element had been largely ignored by Americans, in the military establishment and intelligence services as much as by the civil administration, and the CPA (Coalition Provisional Authority). This last, led then by a contemptuous Paul Bremer, was entirely ideologically driven and disconnected from reality.

The only American who realised there was a game to be played between Iraqi religious communities was probably David Petraeus, the commander of the 101$^{st}$ Airborne who was in charge of occupation troops in Mosul.[3] (He then became commander-in-chief of American troops in Iraq, and after that, director of the CIA.)

Petraeus was an assiduous reader of the French strategist David Galula, who wrote a theory on counter-insurgency warfare during the Algerian war of independence. Petraeus wanted to learn the lessons of French colonial experience. During the 1920s, despite its claims of secularism, France institutionalised ethnic and communitarian divisions in Syria and Lebanon to establish its mandate. Petraeus therefore applied French colonial policy by setting up a Mosul local council based on dividing the city up on community lines. A twenty-four-person assembly reflected the region's ethnic make-up: Sunni Arabs, Kurds, Turkmens, Christians and Yazidis. The press praised his idea as a stroke of genius. There were comments such as: 'At least there's one man who has understood the ethnology of Iraq!'

He did nothing more than to inject a little more sectarian poison into the bloodstream of Iraqi society.

The American occupation forces did not escape the curse whereby the West creates its own enemies in the Middle East

[3] ???

through its mistakes. In fact, two early decisions taken by the US proconsul Paul Bremer as good as guaranteed the birth of the Iraqi insurgency—two executive orders that were effectively colonial decrees.

*Executive order number one*: the dissolution of the Ba'ath Party, and exclusion of all its members from public office. *Executive order number two*: the disbanding of the Iraqi army. De-Ba'athification, although a response to the understandable need to revive Iraq's elites post-Saddam, was in fact an encouragement to nepotism. What was being sought above all was the placement within the state apparatus of a new class close to the new leaders. These leaders almost all originated from the Iraqi diaspora and returned to their country on the invader's coattails. This measure involved the shuffling of far too many people, and made a huge number of civil servants unemployed, though they had shown no particular loyalty to the fallen regime and were necessary for the smooth running of the state.

The disbanding of the army also cast opprobrium on a largely Sunni military elite which the occupiers considered responsible for war crimes, although the army hadn't even fought when American and British troops arrived in Baghdad. Army staff were sent home in dishonour, unemployed at the very moment when Iraq faced a major security challenge; looting on a massive scale was destroying a large portion of the country's infrastructure, from ministries, to high voltage electric cables and pylons, whose metal was being sold on the black market.

During the brutal initial weeks of occupation, the first Iraqi resistance networks took shape. Like a sorcerer's apprentice, the occupying forces had blundered upon the recipe for an explosive Islamist-Ba'athist cocktail. Attacks proliferated. They were at first classified as 'incidents' by the US army:

here a grenade attack on an American patrol, gunshots elsewhere. Guerrilla warfare moved up a gear with the car bomb attack on the Jordanian embassy in early August 2003, and in particular after the explosion destroying the seat of the United Nations on the 19th of that month, claiming the lives of Kofi Annan's special envoy, the Brazilian diplomat Sergio Vieira de Mello. Abu Musab al-Zarqawi claimed responsibility for this attack.[4] In the aftermath, the UN withdrew most of its expatriate staff and drastically reduced its operations. In October, the International Committee of the Red Cross's delegation was targeted. From this moment, the insurgents' gamble had paid off. The international community largely abandoned Baghdad for security reasons or retreated to its bunkers. The insurgents managed to create a vacuum around the occupying forces and henceforth went head to head with the US military. War could commence.

The insurgency flared up in the spring of 2004, as the coalition was about to celebrate the invasion's first anniversary, dissolve the CPA and cede some of its powers to the first provisional Iraqi government. The murder of employees of

---

[4] Michael Weiss and Haddan Hassan, in their book *Isis: Inside the Army of Terror*, quote an American Colonel, Derek Harvey, in charge of fighting the insurgency during the American occupation years. Harvey claims that, 'originally, the Ba'athists cooperated in the bombing of the UN and in other suicide bombings in 2003.' According to him, the Special Security Operation, in charge of Saddam Hussein's Republican Guard and Special Forces, 'provided Zarqawi's men with the cars that were fashioned into VBIEDS; they also transported the suicide bombers.' If indeed there was no collaboration between bin Laden and the Iraqi dictator in the years leading up to the invasion, very early on in the insurgency, it would seem that Ba'athists and Saddam's ex-henchmen worked hand-in-hand first to destabilize the CPA, and then to sow the seeds of a sectarian civil war between Shia and Sunni.

the Blackwater security firm, and above all the humiliation of their bodies being mutilated and displayed, drew the United States into the bloody siege of Fallujah. At the same time, militiamen of the Mahdi Army (the popular and radical Shia movement of Muqtada al-Sadr) opened a second front. Several Westerners were taken hostage, some of whom were murdered. Abu Musab al-Zarqawi was establishing a strategy that would become that of Islamic State.

Politically, the Sunnis fell into the trap of non-participation. Unable to accept their loss of status and the brutality of the exclusions from military and political power, they decided to boycott the first elections. This was a major mistake, since they contributed to their own marginalisation, further stoking the flames of the insurgency. The resistance was also fed by a long list of frustrations: the dismally slow pace of reconstruction, which allowed waste and corruption on a huge scale; the violent sectarianism of the security forces, who even carried out torture in the basement of the Interior Ministry, despite the presence of so many American 'advisors'[5]; and a lack of

---

[5] As mentioned by Michael Weiss and Hassan Hassan, Ibid., in those days when the Shia rose to power in Baghdad, 'a Ministry of Interior uniform conferred authority and impunity on active members of sectarian death squads . . . No single episode better characterised for Sunnis the new republic of fear being constructed atop the ruins of the former one than the Jadriya Bunker. A detention facility situated just south of the Green Zone, the bunker's Special Interrogations Unit was run by Bashir Nasr al-Wandi, nicknamed "Engineer Ahmed". A former senior intelligence operative for the Badr Corps, Engineer Ahmed was seconded to Qassem Suleimani's Quds Force. When US soldiers finally opened the door of this dungeon prison, they found 168 blindfolded prisoners, all of whom had been held there for months, in an overcrowded room filled with faeces and urine. Nearly every prisoner was a Sunni, and many bore signs of

prospects at a time when the economy had ground to a halt and Iraqis still expected the state to be a great provider of jobs.

In just a few years, Iraq descended into hell. Another more radical, violent and anti-Shia movement was added to the 'standard' resistance to occupation. The influence of al-Qaida's Iraqi branch (*Al-Qaida bi-Rafidayn*), led by Abu Musab al-Zarqawi, grew stronger. American troops, who were entrenched, strongly armoured and responded swiftly and forcefully to every attack, were not its main targets. Rather than the US forces, Zarqawi's men preferred to strike mainly Shia civilian targets, to provoke a state of chaos that would bring about more repression and a spiral of violence likely to plunge the population into a state of helplessness. Zarqawi sent more car bombs into markets than mortar shells into American bases, with the clear aim of stoking the flames of sectarian hatred. In this, he was more successful than he could have dreamed.

The attack on the Al-Askari Mosque (the great Shia mausoleum in Samarra) on 22 February 2006 prompted large-scale reprisals. Iraq plunged into civil war. The American army was forced to give up on intervention and focus on building more barriers between urban communities. Baghdad and its suburbs and many large Iraqi cities were fragmented and criss-crossed by 'T-walls'—four-metre high concrete walls separating neighbourhoods and different religious communities. The Americans were fortifying their positions. The Iraqi government, entrenched in the comfort of Baghdad's green zone, was cut off from the country's realities. Al-Qaida's bet was paying off.

Then came the 'surge', the offensive conceived by David Petraeus, to whom George Bush had entrusted command of the

---

torture—some were so badly beaten they had to be taken to the Green Zone for medical treatment.'

expeditionary force in Iraq. The aim was to administer tough medicine: substantial reinforcements were sent to Iraq, where the number of US military personnel reached 150,000. These reinforcements concentrated almost exclusively on the two provinces of Baghdad and Al-Anbar, and were meant to break up the insurgency's structures so that US troops could intervene and prevent inter-communal killings. This was intended in the long run to achieve the conditions that would enable the US to withdraw completely, bathed in glory. However, in addition to sending reinforcements, there was a second component of Petraeus' plan, and it was this which produced the most visible results: agreements were made with local tribes through their sheikhs. These tribes were officially paid to fight al-Qaida. In reality, these were largely groups who belonged to the resistance, and who were receiving a salary from their old enemy in return for stopping fighting. It was a bold tactic, which in itself shows that the insurgency had a weak political base: its motivations were largely economic. In Iraq, where the population was used to state hand-outs, economic liberalisation imposed by the occupier and the government's marginalisation of the Sunnis had deprived these people of resources. The creation of Sahwas ('awakening councils') of Sunni militiamen, had a radical effect on al-Qaida, whose numbers and impact on the ground disappeared like snow in the sun. In any case, realising that you can pay off a stubborn enemy rather than fight him was an innovation in US army ideology. The former solution can be less costly.

Between 2008 and 2011, I often accompanied American troops in Iraq as an embedded journalist. I met soldiers who were well-intentioned, but often naïve or disillusioned, and completely out of sync with realities on the ground. One of their tasks was to train Iraqi soldiers who did not need training.

Military training is not what is most lacking in the Iraqi army. What is missing is allegiance to the state, commitment to defending the nation. This is so seriously lacking that speaking of an Iraqi army is almost a fallacy; it is more like a sectarian-based collection of militiamen. This army remains, more than a decade after its reconstruction, a large and motley patchwork of Shia and Kurdish militias. Moreover, at the moment when the last US troops were leaving Iraq, I was surprised by the ability of Iraqis to be a self-occupying force. Iraqi policemen and soldiers became occupiers in their own country. They took the place of the coalition in the streets, with the same uniforms and equipment, and above all the same behaviour. These security forces took sly pleasure in imitating in all aspects the American army's appearance, habits and even physical mannerisms.

Just as they abandoned their allies in Afghanistan after the Soviet withdrawal, the US has by and large washed its hands of Iraq. What matters, Americans think, is that Obama kept his promise to bring the boys home. For the White House, that's all that counts. The troops' departure, however, was just like the invasion and occupation: botched. The Sunnis, who had been so opposed to occupation, anxiously watched the troops leave. They realised that American policy had, in fact, kept a sectarian and authoritarian prime minister, Nouri al-Maliki, in check. In 2010, in order to disqualify electoral rivals, he restarted a process of 'de-Ba'athification', which the Secretary of State had previously managed to suspend. The process was particularly intended to weaken the non-sectarian al-Iraqiya coalition.[6]

---

[6] Five hundred candidates, almost all Sunni, were prevented from running for office on the grounds that they had worked for Saddam's regime. Iyad Alawi, though Shia himself, was seen as the best bet for the political survival and visibility of the Sunni community.

After the elections, Maliki refused to share power, and took control of the defence and interior ministries. Above all, he methodically dismantled the main inheritance of the US occupation, the Sahwas. The original contract, when the Americans recruited these militias, suggested they would be funded initially by the US taxpayer. The process, however, had to become viable through integration of most of these anti-al-Qaida militiamen into the Iraqi security forces. The hiring of a million Sunnis thus had to be made permanent. Obviously Maliki had no intention of giving political influence back to the Sunnis within his security apparatus; nor did he wish to share state resources beyond his community. Most members of Sahwas were dismissed. Almost ten years after the break-up of the Iraqi army, the Sahwas' *de facto* demobilisation had similar consequences: the marginalised Sunnis became isolated in the political landscape and were tempted to resume the armed struggle and criminal practices.

The French-Iraqi journalist Feurat Alani has described Maliki's increasing isolation, remote in his sectarian authoritarianism. 'Since he mistrusts the Sunnis, he has kept them away from power. But because he also mistrusts the popular Sadrist Shia party, he has tried to play the nationalist card. But this doesn't always work, because it frightens the Kurds. So he uses force to remain in power. Alone against everyone.'[7]

The Arab Spring had special resonance in Baghdad. Here too, the young had democratic aspirations, nurtured by intense interaction on social networks. The younger generation also wants to be free of sectarianism. Maliki, however, reacted

---

[7] Quoted by Warda Mohamed, 'Constat d'échec en Irak', OrientXXI. info, 1 November 2013. Also in Feurat Alani, 'Irak-Syrie, mêmes combats', *Le Monde diplomatique*, January 2014.

despotically. He deployed his arsenal of anti-terrorist legislation to muzzle dissent: government opponents were arrested and imprisoned under state-of-emergency laws; several were sentenced to death, internal travel restrictions were introduced, and foreign media were prohibited from travelling to Al-Anbar province. As the demonstrations grew, the Iraqi security forces, as expected, cracked down on them. The demonstrators from tribes in western Iraq, who at times had been part of the Sahwas but rejected Maliki's sectarianism, were dispersed with live ammunition.

A familiar, and all too predictable, sequence of events followed: democrats were sidelined, the opposition was radicalised, acquired weapons, and then challenged the government and threatened Ramadi and Fallujah. The Sunnis had 'sectarianised' their opposition, opposing Nouri al-Maliki's backing of the repression of the Syrian revolution in the name of Shia solidarity. The government allowed militiamen to travel to Syria to assist the Syrian army and police in their struggle against the revolutionaries. Many of these militiamen belonged to Asaib Ahl al-Haq ('League of the Righteous') and are followers of Muqtada al-Sadr. During 2013, the repression grew harsher and Maliki reacted like Assad: Iraqi army helicopters (which belonged to an institution the Americans claimed to have rebuilt according to principles of democracy and respect for human rights) began bombing civilian areas with barrel bombs. They did this in exactly the same way as Syrian helicopters were doing in Aleppo and the suburbs of Damascus.

It was in these circumstances that Islamic State decided to launch a takeover of Jabhat al-Nusra in spring 2013. A young European jihadi, who was one of my jailers when I was an Islamic State hostage in Raqqa in 2014, tried to explain to me why this operation was legitimate. He claimed that Jabhat al-Nusra was formerly, in Iraq, nothing more than an offshoot of what was Islamic State. He said that the merger came about only when Abu Mohammad al-Julani, the *amir* of al-Qaida's official franchise, made his wish for autonomy too evident.

But the conflict between Abu Bakr al-Baghdadi and Julani (who appealed to Ayman al-Zawahiri and received his backing) shows that this was a competition between two groups which are more rivals than partners. The two movements tried to appear on good terms, even as the split was becoming apparent, and in May 2013 local al-Nusra *emirs* were asked to decide between allegiance to Julani and Islamic State. Divorce in a conservative family, however, is always messy. The two former partners unsurprisingly began to tear each other apart for the spoils and booty, which led to military confrontation that winter. Relations between Jabhat al-Nusra and Islamic State remain complex. They might be characterised as a relationship between competitors, with some fighting, but also occasional alliances. As always, circumstances on the ground dictate behaviour at least as much as leaders' orders.

Abu Bakr al-Baghdadi needs little introduction; he has already been widely profiled in the media. He is believed to have been born in 1971 in Samarra, a city north of Baghdad, and to have graduated in Islamic studies from Baghdad University. He was running the legal committee of the mujahadin Shura Council, a coalition of Iraqi Islamist insurgent groups. The most salient feature of his background is that he was probably imprisoned at Camp Bucca, one of the main American military detention centres in Iraq, in the desert near the Kuwaiti border. Information available (rumours might be a more appropriate term) suggests he was imprisoned either between the months of

February and December 2004 or from 2005 to 2009. Whatever the truth, several high-ranking members of Islamic State would seem to be Camp Bucca 'veterans'.[8] Many jihadists I met had been imprisoned. Even one of the main *emirs* in charge of my captivity—an Iraqi—boasted about his detention during his years of anti-American guerrilla activity. Another of my jailers even claimed to have spent years in Guantanamo. Syrian prisons, as well as the US army's internment camps in Iraq, were for many an effective 'jihad academy'.

Everything changed when large swathes of Iraqi territory fell into Islamic State's hands. The conquest of Mosul, a city taken within a few days in June 2014 after the Iraqi army was routed, was a severe shock. Reuters' Baghdad correspondent, Ned Parker, who has perhaps spent more time in Iraq since the US invasion than any other Western journalist, described the battle for the northern Iraqi city:

> As Islamic State fighters raced towards Mosul before dawn
> on 6 June, the jihadists hoped only to take a neighbourhood

---

[8] Michael Weiss and Hassan Hassan, Ibid., describe the American camp as the perfect 'school for jihadists'. They quote Stone, one of the US officers responsible, who mentions that 'the takfiris were extremely well organised in Bucca; they arranged where their people slept and where they were moved to. . . In fact, one of the large cells was nicknamed Camp Caliphate. . . If you were looking to build an army, prison is the perfect place to do it. We gave them health care, dental, fed them, and, most importantly, we kept them from getting killed in combat. Who needs a safe house in Anbar when there's an American jail in Basra?' Weiss and Hassan quotes another former Islamic State inmate of Camp Bucca as saying: 'We could never have all got together like this in Baghdad, or anywhere else . . . It would have been impossibly dangerous. Here, we were not only safe, but we were only a [few hundred] away from the al-Qaida leadership.'

for several hours, one of them later told a friend in Baghdad. They did not expect state control to crumble. They hurtled into five districts in the hundreds, and would, over the next few days, reach over 2,000 fighters, welcomed by the city's angry Sunni residents. [9]

After a few days' fighting, the soldiers panicked and took flight, abandoning their weapons and even uniforms, in order to leave the city unimpeded.

Feurat Alani has described the reaction of the people of Mosul. Not everyone greeted the jihadists' arrival by throwing flowers. But almost all threw stones at the fleeing Iraqi security forces. Local people allowed Islamic State to gain a foothold more out of frustration than because they supported their views.[10] In Mosul, as in Ramadi, Fallujah and the large Syrian cities, the people had the same feeling: of living under occupation by their own armed forces. These failures of the Iraqi army and police is also extremely serious, because these institutions have lost all trust, including in the communities they come from. Panic spread through Iraq's Shia and Kurdish regions, and also Baghdad. People realised how

[9] Ned Parker, Isabel Coles, Raheem Salman, 'How Mosul fell—An Iraqi general disputes Baghdad's story', Reuters.com, 14 October 2014.

[10] The French scholar and specialist of modern Iraq Pierre-Jean Luizard emphasises in *Le piège Daech: L'Etat Islamique ou le retour de l'Histoire* (The Daesh Trap: Islamic State or the Return of History), that 'one can understand why Islamic State fighters in January in Falloujah, then in June in Tikrit, Mosul and elsewhere are considered by a large proportion of the locals as a liberation army. In all Sunni Arab regions, the Iraqi army was often described as the 'check point army', more experienced in exercising irritating control over the inhabitants' commute, making life truly hell—sometimes several hours were needed to travel a few kilometres—without guaranteeing a minimal level of security.'

weak their armed forces were. Even in communities which were favourable to it, the army lost any residual trust and an emergency mobilisation of sectarian militias took place. Shia militias were mobilised to protect Baghdad and several cities in Diyala to the north-east, while the Kurdish Peshmerga built up their numbers to defend Erbil.

What enabled Islamic State to take Mosul so quickly and easily was the strange opportunistic alliance that it had established with former Ba'athist army officers. Romain Caillet, whose research brings him into regular contact with jihadists, has described the disbelief of foreign volunteers who had fought in Syria (for whom the Ba'ath party was evil incarnate) on seeing how active the old Iraqi Ba'athist networks were within Islamic State on the other side of the border. The insult 'Ba'athist' was sometimes used, at least as a joke, by 'Syrian' Islamic State fighters to refer to their Iraqi comrades. After the jihadists took Mosul, portraits of Saddam Hussein and Izzat Ibrahim al-Duri (his vice-president) began to appear in the city's streets. Al-Duri was one of Saddam's leading henchmen and a senior figure in the anti-American resistance. Surprising images to find next to black Islamic State flags. Once more, the self-fulfilling prophecy was coming true. Nouri al-Maliki had for years claimed the existence of Islamist-Ba'athist plots in order to denigrate his Sunni opponents. The idea of such an alliance was absurd. But in being repeated it became a reality.

Islamic State's capture of Mosul at least had the advantage of pushing Maliki towards the door. Maliki refused to form a government following the April 2014 parliamentary elections and preferred to lead his country into a political crisis rather than risk losing his job. The army's defeat in Mosul in June provided the opportunity to get rid of him at last, even though he had to be offered the post of Vice-President as a consolation prize.

Haider al-Abadi of the al-Dawa party then came to power in Baghdad. He is a conservative Shia Islamist with close links to Iran and scarcely less sectarian than his predecessor. In a sense he is a curious throwback to the beginning of the occupation, since he was Telecoms minister in the first Iraqi government after Saddam's fall. As a sign of good will, he published on his Twitter account a message saying he had 'given the order to the armed forces to cease bombing civilian areas' held by Islamic State. Ned Parker has written that al-Abadi's priority is 'to start to clean and rebuild the Iraqi forces. Abadi has closed the office Maliki used to direct commanders and has quietly retired officers seen as loyal to his predecessor. Purging the security institutions of their sectarianism, money-making schemes and political manoeuvrings will take years.'[11] This clean-up process led to the discovery of 50,000 non-existent soldiers on the Iraqi army's books.

There can be no improvement of the security situation in Iraq, though, without a more inclusive government in Baghdad, a government that takes into account the aspirations of all sectors of the population. Iraqi politicians, like the country's security forces, are part of the problem rather than the solution. This is all the more the case since political speeches—and even the voting system—have until now simply reinforced sectarian, communal and tribal narratives. It is worrying to see that inter-community political groupings, which have tried to make a breakthrough during the various elections, came out of these polls much weakened. Between the parliamentary elections of 2005 and those of 2014, what has become apparent is that politicians are turning

[11] Ned Parker, Isabel Coles, Raheem Salman, 'How Mosul fell—An Iraqi general disputes Baghdad's story', *opus. cit.*

increasingly inwards. They have tried to attract voters not through their convictions or political positions, but by calling upon communal feelings and people's obligation to vote so as to maintain or strengthen their own interests.

In September 2014, Western and Gulf powers met in Paris for a conference on security in Iraq. Opinions were still overwhelmingly influenced by the shock of the first hostage beheadings, and a military campaign was launched. Leaders had to coordinate their efforts to fight against the Islamic State phenomenon following its rediscovery. At the conference, the United States kept pushing its partners to separate the Syrian and Iraqi components of the response to Islamic State. Washington's view was that 'we can't solve all Syria's problems'. Yet this strategy not only ignores the fact that the group controls a substantial part of Syrian territory, but also that Assad's repression was the main catalyst for the group's creation, and remains one of Islamic State's main drivers.

In October, the United States confirmed its 'Iraq first' strategy, and settled for intermittent operations in Syria. Barack Obama played for time with cosmetic measures, such as the dismissal of Defence Secretary Chuck Hagel. The US administration is wary of over-committing to the region, and is aiming to freeze Islamic State's positions with air strikes, halt its progress, and gain some time to recruit, train and arm a force made up of 'moderate rebels' capable of fighting Islamic State. But as we have seen, each passing day sees a decrease in the number of 'moderates' able or willing to fight in our name.

7

# The Kobane Scam

*The defence of minorities is a misleading trap. All of the region's peoples are entitled to security. The 'mobilisation' for minorities—Kurds, Yazidis or Christians—is a form of communalism and promotes sectarianism.*

Patrice Franceschi, a committed journalist with a mission, had been invited for an in-depth interview by France 24, a channel whose director had called upon correspondents to 'openly take sides against the barbarians' of Islamic State. Franceschi had come to launch an appeal to help 'save Kobane',[1] the Kurdish town in northern Syria near the Turkish border. He warned that the Kurds were 'the only really effective bulwark against Islamic State in the region. In addition, we are, as they say, fighting for the same values. They do not understand why we don't do anything. They have established a real democracy in liberated Syrian Kurdistan, with a government, police, an army, and so on . . .'

The idea that we had to make this border town the jihadists' Stalingrad, and above all that we had to help the Kurdish fighters who were defending it, gained general acceptance in

[1] *L'entretien de France 24* ('The France 24 interview'), 18 November 2014.

the West. The appeal of these fighters was all the greater, since they made much of their secularism and put women on the front line—and children too, though this seemed less morally challenging than Islamic State's child soldiers.

But this support raises a real moral problem. First, because the defenders of Kobane were not just any Kurds, but PYD militiamen, the Syrian branch of the PKK, a party run on Stalinist lines. The PYD did a deal with the regime at the start of the revolution. Its set-up is mafia-style and authoritarian. It may be less criminal than its Islamic State opponents, but it still merited its place on the list of terrorist organisations drawn up by—among others—the United States and the European Union.[2] While in Western countries the battle of Kobane is often presented as a struggle between good and evil, many Syrians see it simply as a confrontation between two terrorist groups.

Some are also surprised that the press only uses the Kurdish name 'Kobane' (though in fact it is not even really Kurdish, since it is a corruption of the word 'company', referring to the train which used to stop there in the heyday of the Istanbul-Baghdad railway). Syrians, by contrast, call this place Ayn al-Arab (the 'spring of the Arabs', because nomads and their flocks would stop there to drink before the arrival of steam locomotives). The jihadists, never slow in the PR war, have renamed the city Ayn al-Islam (the 'spring of Islam'), though there is no mention of this location in religious texts.

While Syrian democrats have never been truly successful in mobilising Western public opinion, this sudden surge of sympathy seems suspect to them, to say the least, if not

---

[2] By contrast with the PKK, which is an 'armed party', the PYD only had a political branch until the onset of the Syrian revolution.

downright biased. Ayman Abdel-Nour was angered by 'the PR campaign around Kobane [which] is entirely conceived to serve interests which have nothing to do with the Syrian revolution. There are—and there have been—massacres more bloody than those in Kobane, and the world has not reacted at all. We respect the Kurds, their culture, their aspirations, but this is too blatant a case of double standards. We have to intervene against all massacres, all over Syria.' The scale of the solidarity movement for the besieged city has also shocked the historian Farouk Mardam-Bey:

> What happened for Kobane is the greatest demonstration of support for Syria we've seen since the revolution began. Mobilising for Kobane is justified, but this is out of proportion in comparison to all the massacres perpetrated previously, which have never raised such international outrage.

Salem Hassan, a Kurdish activist now exiled in Paris, emphasises that 'we are Kurdish, but above all we are Syrians and democrats. Now Abdallah Öcalan appealed to Bashar from his Turkish jail, at the start of the revolution. There are 4,000 Peshmerga based in Iraq, but the PYD won't let them go to Kobane. It wants to keep its monopoly.' As I was interviewing him, he took out his mobile phone and scrolled through photographs of militiamen training, by way of confirmation. The most shocking thing is that the town's population has been taken hostage in this conflict. 'What they want to turn Kobane into is a Stalingrad. But what I see above all is that the city has been turned into a pile of ruins. 250,000 people used to live there. They've all had to leave. They've lost their homes!'

In November 2014, Sam Dagher published an article in the *Wall Street Journal* after a visit to Syria's Kurdish areas.[3] It seems from his interviews that if the PYD suggested cooperating with the West in its struggle against Islamic State, it was in exchange for at least de facto recognition of the autonomous administration this party had set up in North Syria. This is an administration with its own law courts, which has begun to decree its own laws, levy taxes and even distribute specific number-plates.

The PYD is an authoritarian party with a personality cult around its leader Abdullah Öcalan, who has been imprisoned in Turkey since 1999. Billboards and posters with Öcalan's image, visible in barracks and checkpoints under the group's control, declare 'there is no life without the leader.' Dagher recalls that 'since late 2011, with encouragement and support from Iran—Assad's main backer—the PKK and its Syrian Kurdish followers agreed to avoid clashes with the regime in exchange for more power in Kurdish-dominated areas of northern Syria.' This collaboration with a regime, which has relentlessly marginalised the Kurds for as long as it has ruled, provoked tensions with other revolutionary groups, leading to clashes with the Free Syrian Army, as well as Jabhat al-Nusra.

In summer 2013 the PYD drove rebel groups out of the border town of Ras al-Ayn. This was, for the revolutionaries, a new form of betrayal by a group whose murky links to the regime were constantly under criticism. The Kurds' aim is to create a continuum along the Syrian-Turkish border to link the three areas the regime has ceded to them: Afrin to the

---

[3] Sam Dagher, 'Kurds fight Islamic State to claim a piece of Syria', *Wall Street Journal*, 12 November 2014.

north-west of Aleppo, Kobane, and the area extending from Ras al-Ayn to Qamishli in the Jazira.

The political plan was devised by PYD leader Saleh Muslim who himself comes from Kobane. He had been in exile in Iraqi Kurdistan following detention in Syria, where he had been imprisoned with his wife. In 2011, just a few weeks after the revolution began, the regime permitted him to return to Qamishli and did a deal with him. It was a more or less tacit power-sharing and non-aggression pact. Assad urgently needed to freeze the Kurdish front, when his main challengers are Arab Sunnis. In the streets of both Qamishli and Hassake, there are often militiamen brandishing the regime's flag alongside *Asayesh* (PYD police forces). Under the deal, the regime delegated to the Syrian PKK branch the management of the territory it was holding, which has become *de facto* autonomous; in exchange, the Kurds would keep out of the revolution and prevent dissent from taking root in the region.

Bassam al-Ahmad is a Kurd as well as a leader in the Violations Documentation Center NGO in Syria. He explains:

> The PYD is an armed group with its own agenda. They have their policy, which is not what you would expect. They also commit many human rights violations. We are fighting for a free Syria. I come from Qamishli. I know people in the PYD leadership. Some are friends and I criticise them, telling them they often behave exactly like the regime. Most Syrian-Kurdish human rights activists have had to leave their homes and are now living in exile in Europe or Turkey.

Salem Hassan confirms 'the PYD is like the Ba'ath party. Its skeleton is the intelligence services. And it has no popular base; none of the demonstrations the PYD has organised has been able to muster more than a few thousand people.'

In other words, the PYD has a poor reputation among Syrian democrats. They remember that freezing the Kurdish front has allowed Assad to deploy his forces elsewhere. The PYD has little popular support, even among Syrian Kurds. So what is its secret? How has it strengthened its reputation, especially in our own media? Probably by being long established in the West, through the substantial Kurdish diaspora. The PKK has always been very shrewd in displaying its 'socialism', and presents itself as a victim of Cold War logic, combined with dyed-in-the-wool secularism. As a result, old Stalinists have been able to portray themselves as democrats.

The political scientist Ziad Majed told me scathingly how he finds it 'quite odd that a section of those who, among the European Left, have demonstrated against a possible "imperialist intervention" in Syria, when the United States and France were threatening military action after the Ghouta chemical massacre, have remained silent, or even demonstrate today when it comes to defending Kobane, something which has been above all done with US air support. This is more than schizophrenia, this is ethical decline, for I think that if it were Assad's regime attacking Kobane, they would not be in favour of American support for the brave defenders of this Kurdish Syrian city.' The dissident Yassin al-Haj Saleh does not mince words when it comes to describing our so-called 'solidarity with Kobane': 'they want to give us lessons on Kobane! This is ethnocentrism! Sectarianism! You are fighting alongside a terrorist group, and at the same time you've abandoned an entire people!' While the battle for Kobane went on, publisher Farouk Mardam Bey arranged a meeting in Paris about the Kurdish question in Syria, a sensitive issue debated by two eminent Kurds in front of a largely Arab or pro-Arab audience. The political scientist Hamit Bozarslan attempted to show that Iran and Turkey shared great responsibility in making the region increasingly sectarian. He expressed particular disappointment with 'Erdogan's Turkey, which does not understand why the countries of the region do not respond positively to his dreams of empire.'[4]

Sêvê Aydin Izouli, a human rights lawyer and a former representative of the Damascus Declaration, sketched out the history of the widening gap between Arabs and Kurds. Originally there was the absurd 'Arab belt' project. To prevent Kurdish territorial continuity and thwart Syrian Kurds' demands for a state, the regime confiscated a strip of their land 350 kilometres long and 15 kilometres wide. Arab peasants were settled in this zone, in a form of colonialism modelled on Israeli settlement of Palestinian-occupied territory. The Arabs in this area were given military training and weapons. The fault line widened in 2004, during a football game in the Qamishli stadium, when a Kurdish team met an Arab one. Tempers were running high because of the invasion of neighbouring Iraq. Fans started shouting: 'Down with Barzani!' or 'Down with Assad!' The match ended with a fight between rival groups. The Arab fans had apparently been allowed to enter the stadium with sticks and knives, while the Kurds were searched and disarmed. By evening, several people were dead. Predictably, the Kurds' funerals the following day turned into a demonstration. The authorities fired on the crowd. This ignited Kurdish Jazira, but in Damascus the opposition stayed silent. In 2011, when the revolution broke out, the memory of the 2004 Kurdish intifada was very much

[4] Conference of 30 November 2014.

in people's minds. Much time and effort will be needed to reconcile Syria's Kurds and Arabs.

The other minority whose situation causes public outcry in the West is the Christians. In summer 2014, after Islamic State captured Mosul, and with more and more villages falling to the jihadists, a solidarity movement with Middle Eastern Christians attracted a great deal of support in the West, especially on social networks. One of the noteworthy initiatives was the campaign #LightForIraq, which encouraged Internet users to post photographs of candles. Another initiative was started by the Iraqi journalist Dalia al-Aqidi, whose campaign was based on the Arabic letter ن ("*noun*").

At first, this letter had a negative connotation as it was used by jihadists to indicate houses abandoned by Christians, which could be looted and taken by Muslims. In Salafi usage, *nun* represents the first letter of the word Nazarene ('*Nasrani*'), a pejorative term for Christians. Dalia al-Aqidi, an Arab Sunni journalist from Mosul, was shocked by this stigmatisation. She began to wear the cross and to spread around the letter *nun* (a reversal of this stigma), as part of a campaign called 'We are all Christians', which promoted religious tolerance. The two *nun* of the campaign in Arabic (*kuluna masihiyun*) are written in a calligraphy recalling the spray paint used by jihadists to tag Christian homes.

In an interview with Lebanon's *An-Nahar* newspaper, the courageous journalist explained the reasons for her campaign: 'Religious pluralism is a reality in Iraq, the cradle of civilisation, science and culture. Who would benefit from history and civilisation if we went back to the dark ages? Christians belong in this country, and we cannot progress without them or in the absence of part of Iraq.' She also responded bluntly to supporters of *takfir*, the Muslim equivalent of excommunication, which jihadists are fond of, especially to justify the murder of fellow Muslims: 'To those who accuse others of being infidels, I say: you are the non-believers, the apostates, the pagans, you are the head-hunters. I am a simple human being who is defending the children of my country, regardless of their origin or identity.'

I had the chance to meet Dalia al-Aqidi in Beirut a month after she launched her campaign. She was astonished when I told her the extent to which it had gone viral on social media, at least in France. She was also shocked to hear that the extreme right, the nationalists, and all sorts of frustrated people had distorted her initiative for their own racist and islamophobic ends. We joked that we should launch a new campaign, one called "*mim*" (م), a letter which Christians (*masihiyyûn*) and Muslims (*muslimun*) have in common. It is worth noting that at the time of writing, the letter *nun* has gone from her Twitter and Facebook profiles.

Are Syria's Christians really being persecuted by jihadists? The researcher Ayman Jawad al-Tamimi published a provocatively titled study that invited readers to 'separate truth from fiction' in the case of Syria's Christians.[5] First, he highlighted the systematic exaggeration—for political reasons, and due to a convergence of most players' interests—of the number of Christians in Syria. Though the figure of 10 per cent of the population is often quoted, the real figure is, according to him, certainly closer to 5 per cent. He went on to review the incidents reported by media and human rights activists and networks. His conclusion was unequivocal: 'There is nothing to suggest

---

[5] Ayman Jawad al-Tamimi, 'Christians in Syria: Separating Facts from Fiction', 13 November 2012.

the existence of an organised campaign of militant Islamic persecution of Christians throughout Syria.' He acknowledged that 'Christians have been subjected to religiously motivated violence', but not to a greater extent than other Syrian religious communities. Tamimi warns of 'disinformation' about the fate of Syrian Christians and advocates that we do not let ourselves be 'taken in by pro-Assad propaganda outlets which are adept at exploiting Western concerns about the status of Christians for their own ends.'

Even jihadists try to guard against descending into an excess of sectarian violence, which they know could be counter-productive. Thus in the 'Strategic Plan to Reinforce the Political Position of the Islamic State of Iraq', published online in 2010, Islamic State's precursors emphasised the importance of not persecuting Christians. In Raqqa, a *dhimma* pact of 'protection' for minorities in Muslim lands—in exchange for a tax called *jizya*—was offered to Christians in February 2014. This pact forbids theft from and attacks on Christians, their houses and their churches, and protects against those who would try to forcibly convert them.

On the other hand, Christians are subject to a list of constraints which seek to prevent any form of proselytising: they are forbidden from building or rebuilding religious Christian sites, wearing crosses visibly, praying in a way that their neighbours might see, ringing church bells, acting in an aggressive way against Islamic State and harbouring spies or enemies, denigrating Islam or preventing a fellow Christian from converting to Islam. They cannot carry weapons. Though the agreement permits Christians to eat pork and drink alcohol, it must be done in private and in any case, it is really only a theoretical dispensation, since, like tobacco, alcohol is in practice banned and considered a drug by the Islamic police in charge of pursuing 'vice'. In addition, Christians are obliged to pay a hefty *jizya* twice a year.

This pact has not really been put into practice. First because most Christians fled early on, when the jihadists seized Raqqa. And also because the militiamen on the ground are much less subtle than their commanders, since the latter care more about appearing respectable. In fact, seven months after the publication of this *dhimma* decree, Raqqa's two churches were desecrated. The crosses on their towers were taken down. One of these Christian places of worship was converted into a centre for preaching by Islamic State. Of course such desecration is unacceptable, but it is worth remembering that hundreds and even thousands of mosques have been desecrated or destroyed since the Syrian conflict began. There is nothing worse than a victimisation contest and selective outrage. Beyond sectarian propaganda of the various parties, what needs to be re-established above all is tolerance. In April 2015, the Syrian network for Human rights (SNHR) published a report on the destruction of churches since March 2013. It found that out of sixty-three churches damaged, forty had been destroyed by the regime and 'only' seven by Islamic State.

'Daesh massacres indiscriminately,' said Peter Harling, the regional manager of the International Crisis Group, in an interview with the French weekly *Le Point*. 'But its fighters have also carried out mass executions among Sunni Arab tribes, and no one has said a word. They have also beheaded many Alawi soldiers. Not to mention the other horrors perpetrated by players who pay no price for their crimes: the Syrian regime has caused the deaths by malnutrition of many civilians, including children, in neighbourhoods deliberately besieged for this purpose. Anyway, I cannot really see how air strikes against Daesh, divorced from any measures to relieve the other terrible sufferings afflicting the region, will guarantee the future of Christians or of Yazidis.'[6]

Thomas Pierret points out that:

> In the case of Syria, one should add there is an unhealthy focus on the question of minorities, which is reminiscent of colonial rhetoric in the nineteenth century. Supporting Assad in the name of protecting minorities is both immoral and stupid. It is immoral because it makes the protection of minorities acceptable justification for the massacre of tens of thousands of civilians, the razing of entire cities and the displacement of millions of people by the regime: put differently, it values a Christian or Alawi life higher than a Sunni's. It is also completely stupid because, by reinforcing the association between the regime and religious minorities in Sunnis' minds, the current situation puts the future of minorities in danger. What we have to remember is that independent of the battle that is currently being fought, demographic trends mean that Assad's regime is fated to disappear in years or decades to come: religious minorities do not represent more than 20 per cent of the population and their rate of demographic growth is approximately half of that of the Sunni majority. It could be argued that Assad has Sunni support—which is true—but he has been unable to integrate them into his military apparatus to any significant extent. What this regime needs for long-term survival are men ready to die to defend it. The importance of foreign Shia units in the regime's battle tactics speaks volumes about the personnel problems it has had for a long time.

[6] http://www.lepoint.fr/monde/ce-que-cache-la-menace-etat-islamique-26-09-2014-1866999_24.php

Let us look finally to the wisdom of Paolo Dall'Oglio, a Jesuit priest who lived in Syria for decades. A lover of freedom and tolerance, he describes in his book how he used to joke with jihadist fighters when he travelled with them in Idlib province during regime bombings.[7] The priest knew who the Christians' real enemy was. He also knew that repressing the majority is probably the worst way of defending minorities' rights. His wisdom must be reflected upon, even if his trust has been betrayed.

*Abuna* Paolo has disappeared, abducted by Islamic State.

---

[7] Paolo Dall'Oglio, *La Rage et la Lumière*, l'Atelier, Paris, 2013.

# 8

# The Dabiq Miracle

*International intervention is a recruitment sergeant for Islamic State. It turns its apocalyptic prophesy into reality. Intervention weakens the moderate opposition and has contributed to growing sectarianism in the region.*

Barack Obama has done all he can to disengage from the Middle East. His stance has been almost a matter of principle, the basis of his mandate, a political position. It was a visceral reaction to his predecessor's interventions. Whereas George Bush's attitude always seemed to be: 'let's go in', his successor's is 'let's get out'. Faced with genuine international will to do something in Syria, led by France, after the chemical bombings of the Ghouta in Damascus's suburbs, and despite the green light from his administration, Obama himself took the decision not to intervene. This was a knee-jerk anti-Bush reaction.

But the murders of James Foley and Steven Sottloff forced him to react (even before Peter Kassig was killed). With unconvincing bellicosity, he declared, 'The United States will do all with our friends and allies to degrade and ultimately destroy the terrorist group known as ISIL.'[1]

---

[1] Televised speech broadcast from the White House, 10 September 2014.

What Obama overlooked was that by launching his war, he would in the process make the predictions—or indeed the wishes—of jihadists come true. Why has the Syrian jihad been so successful in recruiting foreign fighters?

Undoubtedly because this part of the world is easy to get to for many Arabs and Westerners. Turkey is extremely well connected to the rest of the planet (Turkish airlines has more links to other countries than any rival company); many nationalities can go there without a visa; Turkey, in addition, has long neglected to monitor its borders. The regime's crimes, the horrors most young people have watched unfold on their computer screens and scrolled through on their social media timelines, probably also played a significant part. And finally, the West's inability to intervene, to make international law prevail (the international law that it is so swift in taking into its own hands and twisting when it is for the defence of its own interests), has certainly fostered the idea among would-be jihadists that the international community was at best an accomplice, if not a co-author, of a crime against all Sunni Muslims.

However, one of the strongest points in favour of recruitment, without doubt, derives from the 'Dabiq prophecy'. Dabiq is a small town not much bigger than a village, with around 3,000 inhabitants, located close to the Turkish border north of Aleppo. But it is famous for its place in traditional eschatology. It is the supposed location of *Malahim*, Islam's Armageddon, as expressed in Abu Hureyra's *hadith*, a saying of the Prophet considered authentic (*sahih*):

> The time of Judgement Day will not come to pass before the Rum [Byzantines, thus Christians in jihadists' minds] set up camp at al-Amaq or Dabiq. Then an army from Medina, among the best of the Earth at the time, will go to meet them

in battle. When the two armies are face to face, the Rum will say: 'Leave us by ourselves to fight those who have taken prisoners from us!'—'No, by Allah!' will the Moslems answer! 'We shall never leave you alone with our brothers.'

Upon this refusal, hostilities will begin. A third, whom God will never forgive, will be routed. A third, the best martyrs for Allah, will perish. A third, which will never be tested (or troubled), will gain victory, and will conquer Constantinople.

During the sharing of booty, when swords will hang from olive trees, a demon will cry among them: 'The Antichrist has gone to your homes!' They will break camp, leaving everything behind them, even though the information is false. However, when they walk over the lands of Sham, he [the Antichrist] will truly come out. While preparing for battle, at the very moment the fighters will join ranks, the call for prayer will resound.

In the midst of this event, Jesus, son of Mary, will descend from the Sky and shall lead the prayers. When God's enemy has seen him, he will melt like salt in water. Were he to be left like this, he would dissolve totally until he disappears, but God will make him die between his hands, in order to expose the enemy's blood on a spear.

The following far more effective if much less lyrical prophecy was attributed to Abu Musab al-Zarqawi: 'The flame was lit in Iraq and it will increase with Allah's permission until the Crusader armies are burnt at Dabiq.'[2] Many jihadists have got it into their heads that the battle of the end of the world—what Muslims call *malahim*—will take place in Dabiq and

---

[2] Every issue of *Dabiq*, the magazine published by Islamic State, opens with this quote from Zarqawi.

result in the permanent and final victory of the Muslims over the 'Romans'.

Dabiq as apocalypse and Armageddon is one of Islamic State's strongest brands. It is the name of its English language online magazine. It also features in one of the most atrocious videos published to this day by Islamic State's media arm, called 'Whether Unbelievers Like It or Not'. The final scene, showing the severed head of the American hostage Peter Kassig at his executioner's feet was filmed in Dabiq. In spite of the group's apparent adherence to this end-times narrative, in recent videos the tormentor blamed the West for having invaded Muslim land, and threatened his hostages with reprisals if the United States and Great Britain did not end their intervention and remove their military hardware. In this video, the mask finally falls and Islamic State's double-speak is revealed: what Islamic State wants is not the end of Western military interventions, but the opposite: it wants to provoke them. This time the man nicknamed Jihadi John almost invites the US army in and warns that it will meet its end at Dabiq. 'Here we are,' he says to the camera, 'burying the first American Crusader at Dabiq. Waiting impatiently for the rest of your armies . . .'

The journalist David Thomson told me about the wonder he saw in the eyes of some jihadists, with whom he is in contact for his research, when the international air strikes began. Some of these youths were tiring of combat and were exhausted by the fratricidal struggles with other Islamist factions. But when the West's intervention began, the prophecy, the Dabiq miracle, was being fulfilled! Their motivation redoubled, as did their conviction of being in the right. Dabiq has entered legend, kept alive particularly on social media. A French jihadist, who is one of the most active converts on the Internet, posted on his Twitter account a sentence in peculiar French spelling whose

English equivalent would be: 'The Prophet SAWS [Arabic letters spelling out Peace and Prayer upon Him] as sayd at Dabiq there wil be so many corps that the birds flying over Dabiq will dy coz of the smel.' One English-speaking jihadist wrote: 'Dabiq will happen, this is for sure. The US and their allies will come to Syria once they have seen their air campaign is doomed to failure. It is a promise of God and of his Prophet.' Each day tens, if not hundreds, of tweets are sent to promise that the 'lions of Islam' will soon have the opportunity to confront the crusaders at Dabiq.

It is worth remembering the media rhetoric when the international intervention began in late summer 2014. Islamic State was not only spoken of as the embodiment of evil, but also as an imminent threat to all people in the region, and to the Middle East's very stability. As a result, this intervention had widespread public support. It was nevertheless based on a fallacy, peddled as much by our media as our politicians: after taking control of Mosul, Iraq's second city, Islamic State was considered to be on the verge of seizing Erbil and even Baghdad. Perhaps it is worth repeating that Islamic State is primarily an insurgent group and, as such, can only establish itself in regions where it can find local (Sunni) allies.

Islamic State was certainly able to inflict heavy losses on the northern Iraqi Peshmerga, but it is ridiculous and even counter-productive to claim it could take Erbil. The narrative of the Iraqi Kurdish authorities ('The United States and Europe saved us'), even if it does flatter our egos, is not only propaganda, but also contributes to Islamic State's PR by exaggerating Islamic State's abilities. Erbil is inhabited almost exclusively by Kurds, and it is a powerful metropolis Islamic State cannot take and will never be able to control.

As for Baghdad, the second most populous city in the Arab world, largely purged of its Sunni population, it is ludicrous to think that Islamic State could ever conquer it. This does not mean it could not take control of its Sunni suburbs. Nor does it mean that it lacks allies and a capacity for harassment. Islamic State, for as long as its guerrilla warfare against the Iraqi government lasts, will continue to set off car bombs in the middle of Shia neighbourhoods, perpetuating its strategy of terror and chaos. And it is probably capable of carrying out abductions and murders in the centre of the capital. But saying that it will one day be capable of 'taking Baghdad' simply falls into Islamic State's propaganda trap. But such talk was very common when our politicians were mobilising opinion to justify the air strikes.

This dramatic way of presenting the Islamic State threat, a threat associated with the very real routing of the Iraqi army in all Sunni areas, increased sectarian instincts at a time when the population's respect for the Iraqi army was reaching an all-time low. The great Ayatollah Ali al-Sistani played an important role in the mobilisation of grassroots Shia fighters. When Mosul fell, he issued a fatwa calling for Iraqis 'to defend their country, its people, the honour of its citizens and its sacred sites'. As soon as news of this fatwa spread, hundreds of thousands of volunteers rushed to militia recruitment centres.

Ghaith Abdul-Ahad, a journalist of Iraqi origin, wrote a remarkable account in the *Guardian* of Shia fighters' emergency mobilisation, supposedly to protect the capital against Islamic State.[3] He describes the massacres committed by these militias who 'consider all Sunnis their enemy'. He quotes Moujtaba,

[3] Gaith Abdul-Ahad, 'On the Frontline with the Shia fighters taking the war to Isis', *Guardian*, 24 August 2014.

one of these young militiamen, who is not yet thirty years old,
but who had already travelled to Syria to support Bashar al-
Assad's regime. Moujtaba admitted that:

> You can't depend on the army—even if they put 2,000
> soldiers in this village I won't take them seriously or count
> on them. We are a resistance faction that have been fighting
> for eleven years. Each one of us has been sent to at least
> three outside training camps in Iran and Lebanon under
> the supervision of Hezbollah. Each lasted for two months.
> Do you know what it means to go for sixty days under
> constant grilling by Hezbollah? You come back as a new
> person. You can't compare us with those soldiers who joined
> the army for money.

Donatella Rovera, Amnesty International's special advisor
on crisis response, travelled to northern Iraq after the coalition's
air strikes. She saw how this intervention was followed by
sectarian violence on the ground, which widened the divide
between religious communities. The counter-offensive led by
the Iraqi government, with the support of Westerners and
the backing on the ground of Shia and Kurdish militias, was
marked by a long series of abuses. She says:

> You should see the locations which have been retaken by
> the Shia militias who were fighting against Islamic State ... I
> have been to about forty villages. They have been thoroughly
> destroyed. It is clear now that the inhabitants will not be able
> to return in the foreseeable future. The Sunni population is
> collectively accused of having collaborated with Islamic State.
> Its members have been displaced, chased out of their homes.
> What can they do now?

It appears obvious that some of them, victimised because of being Sunni, will seek refuge with Islamic State, which in their eyes offers the most secure protection against what they consider Shia expansionism. Rovera goes on:

> The same happened in the north where the Peshmerga regained ground; they destroyed everything. The Arabs cannot return. Everything has been destroyed. People have been expelled from their homes, they're prohibited from entering the Kurdish areas and they can only seek refuge in Mosul. They are being pushed towards Islamic State.

The fight against Sunni Islamist terrorism also provided Shia militias and many elements in the Iraqi government with the excuse to cleanse Baghdad and its suburbs of Sunnis and refugees who had fled the 'Sunni triangle' as a consequence of the severe fighting. These justifications were in particular voiced by Hakem al-Zameli, the head of the Iraqi Parliament's Security and Defence Committee, who told Al-Sumaria TV on 21 April 2015 that 'hundreds of displaced Sunni families from Mosul and Tikrit were recruited by Islamic State to penetrate security in Baghdad under the pretext of displacement.'

The Iraqi journalist Ahmad Jabbar Gharib insisted the opposite was the case. In an interview with *Al-Monitor*, he says that he can confirm that those displaced in 2003 were genuine refugees. He believes that the people were forced to migrate, and that the forced displacement happening today was caused in the first place by Islamic State attacks on densely populated Sunni cities such as Fallujah, Ramadi and areas west of Baghdad:. 'The people of Anbar are forced to flee to Baghdad and Shia areas that surround their province, as they have no other refuge, especially since other surrounding areas are deserts that are not suitable to live in.'

The Iraqi government sent a disastrous message when they invited Qassem Suleimani to their country. The chief of Iran's al-Quds force, an elite unit, appears to have arrived 'at the head of a group of Lebanese experts and Iranian soldiers', shortly after Islamic State's seizure of Mosul on 10 July, according to the pro-Iranian Shia Lebanese channel al-Manar.[4] His first mission was to 'make Baghdad and its surroundings secure', then 'to secure the road linking Baghdad to Samarra'. According to Hezbollah's television channel, Suleimani 'took part in the main battles against Islamic State in the Western region of al-Anbar, the Kurdish areas of the Diyala, the oil-producing area of Kirkuk and during the recent battle for the Baiji refinery.'[5]

Qassem Suleimani was the Iranian envoy to Iraq. He was entrusted with ensuring the failure of the US's occupation of Iraq after the 2003 invasion. With his deputy Abu Mahdi al-Muhandis, an Iraqi who had spent the 1980s in Iran and who was linked to the 1983 bombing of the US embassy in Kuwait, he made sure American troops suffered chaos and mayhem. Michael Weiss and Hassan Hassan describe how Muhandis 'was selected to oversee trafficking one of the deadliest weapons ever used in the Iraq War: a roadside bomb known as the explosively formed penetrator, or EFP for short. When detonated, the heat from the EFP melts the copper housing of

[4] 'Iranian commander led anti-jihadist counter-attack in Iraq: Hezbollah', AFP, 28 November 2014.
[5] Ibid.

the explosive, turning it into a molten projectile that can cut through steel and battle armour, including tank walls. The US military reckoned that these devices constituted 18 per cent of all coalition combat deaths in the last quarter of 2006. They were manufactured in Iran and smuggled across the border by Iranian agents working with the Badr Corps, then used by all manner of Shia militias, earning them the sobriquet of "Persian bombs".[6]

Suleimani had been so successful in causing trouble for the Americans, via Shia militias and his al-Quds brigade, that General Petraeus labelled one of Teheran's proxies, Moqtada Sadr's Mahdi Army, as 'more of a hindrance to long-term security in Iraq than al-Qaida'.

Suleimani is also the man who in 2008 sent a text message to General Petraeus, then commander-in-chief of American forces in Iraq, saying, 'Dear General Petraeus, you should know it is me, Qassem Suleimani, who dictates the Iranian Islamic Republic's policy in Iraq, in Lebanon, in Gaza and in Afghanistan.'[7] The Major-General was put in charge of the Syrian file shortly after the revolution began. The fact that he was sent by Tehran to coordinate the struggle against Islamic State is an illustration of the acute sectarian polarisation of this conflict. On the level of regional geopolitics, Islamic State can be interpreted as a reaction of the Sunni world to a fear (in fact very probably exaggerated by its Gulf sponsors) to the growth of the 'Shia crescent'.[8] Sending Suleimani to Iraq

---

[6] Michael Weiss and Hassan Hassan, Ibid., pp. 52-53.

[7] As told by Armin Arefi, 'Le nouvel 'ami' iranien des Etats-Unis', *Le Point*, 31 August 2014.

[8] The expression is from King Abdullah of Jordan who in 2006 was dreading the instauration of a new geopolitical axis linking Iran

played a significant part in this escalation of tension between the Sunni and Shia worlds.

Of course, the boasts of some Iraqi Shia, for whom the absorption of Iraq into Iran is a matter of pride, are of little help in quelling the fears of Iraq's Sunni minority. Sunnis have grown accustomed to thinking since Saddam Hussein's war against Iran that the Persians, and Shia, are 'majous' (Magi wizard heretics). It is important to realise how frightening the dissemination of certain videos such as the one which shows an Iranian fighter with a Kalashnikov slung over his shoulder and a picture of Khamenei pinned to his chest are for Sunnis. This Iranian militiaman brags about Teheran's role in the campaign for Tikrit in the Sunni Triangle: 'I'm proud to participate in the battle to liberate Tikrit.' Calling himself Sheikh Dawood, he adds decisively: 'Iran and Iraq are one state now.' These words do little to dispel the now widespread narrative of two blocks, Sunni and Shia, fighting for the spoils of regional states.

Also a source of major discomfort and fear for Sunnis, as well as for all those still believing in the necessity of an independent and sovereign Iraqi State, is the fact that during the Battle of Tikrit, Iraqi army troops, not numbering more than 4,000, were completely outnumbered by Shia militias (10,000 strong). Much publicised revenge killings also act against the success of a counter-offensive against Islamic State. Murders in Tikrit at the hands of Shia paramilitaries

---

with Lebanon, passing through Syria and Iraq, now governed by the Shia. It was an expression stigmatizing the tensions between the Sunni and the Shia worlds. Of course, it provoked a reaction of outrage in Baghdad.

feed into the narrative of the Sunnis, who now perceive themselves as a community fighting for survival in Iraq. Ned Parker, the Reuters reporter who had to leave the country as a result of threats on his life by Shia militias, has described how 'since its recapture, the Sunni city of Tikrit has been the scene of violence and looting. In addition to the killing of the extremist combatant, Reuters correspondents also saw a convoy of Shi'ite paramilitary fighters—the government's partners in liberating the city—drag a corpse through the streets behind their car.'[9] At more or less the same time, Ahmed al-Kraim, head of the Salahuddin (Tikrit) Provincial Council, told Reuters that mobs had burned down 'hundreds of houses' and looted shops over the previous two days. As CIA chief John Brennan said recently, what this campaign of revenge amounts to is wasting and squandering opportunities the Iraqi government had after reconstituting 'to put at rest some of these sectarian tensions and ... be more inclusive as far as bringing the Sunni community in.'[10]

It is still too early to say whether Iraq will be able to heal its wounds by bridging the Shia–Sunni divide. It looks like an impassable hurdle and makes the country's survival as a united state unlikely.

In diplomacy, as in many other fields, a knee-jerk reaction is never a good thing. In September 2014 François Hollande decided to involve France in air strikes in Iraq after French hostage Hervé Gourdel's killing in Algeria. This stand makes

---

[9] Ned Parker, 3 April 2015, 'Special Report: After Iraqi forces take Tikrit, a wave of looting and lynching' http://www.reuters.com/article/2015/04/03/us-mideast-crisis-iraq-tikrit-special-re-idUSKBN0MU1DP20150403

[10] Fox News interview, 22 March 2015.

no sense. In an interview with *Le Point*, Peter Harling, regional officer of the International Crisis Group, said that 'announcing you will avenge a murder which happened in Algeria in Iraq or elsewhere belongs to show politics, public relations, and is not a real strategy'.[11]

Harling is worth quoting again to elucidate the ambiguous relationship between the Sunni Arab population and Islamic State:

> The Sunni Arab world is going through an existential crisis of sorts. The region has, so to speak, missed the boat when it comes to putting behind it the era of regression that characterised it under the Ottoman Empire's domination, a domination that gave way to colonialism, Western interference in everything and the traumatic creation of Israel. The great emancipating movements, which were at first immense sources of inspiration, rapidly degenerated into autocratic and kleptomaniac cliques. Their Islamist alternatives, which articulated various seductive yet utopian visions of the future, failed miserably when it came to putting theory into practice.
>
> The Arab Spring—this brilliant, splendid moment of inspiration, which could have offered the region redemption and a fresh start—also ended in disaster, leading to a sense of confusion, failure, bitterness, injustice and humiliation. Add to this the unimaginable violence coming out of the Syrian regime, without any serious reaction from the West. Also add the scale of the humanitarian crisis that followed. Add the

[11] Peter Harling, 'Ce que cache la menace 'Etat Islamique', *lepoint. fr*, 26 September 2014.

pathetic spectacle provided by reactionary currents in Egypt, the Gulf and elsewhere. Add finally the constant provocations from the Shia world which—having been marginalised for decades—now sees a chance for a historical revenge, under the form of an imperial influence across the region. In the end, very few people like Islamic State, but that is all there is.

Belgian journalist Baudouin Loos wrote an op-ed in Brussel's daily *Le Soir*, calling on the West not to fall into what he calls 'the beheadings trap':[12]

> The bigger and more brutal the West's reactions, the more these jihadists from hell will think they are increasing the Sunni Muslim world's awareness by emphasising the powerful feeling of 'double standards', since it is true that the international community has for three years watched with total passivity the martyrdom of an entire people: the Syrian Sunni majority. And these jihadists have decided to exploit such a feeling of injustice to recruit and convince.

A Western intervention that only hits the jihadists and does not touch the regime that is massacring Sunnis makes Sunnis feel worse than abandoned: they feel surrounded. On 19 November 2014, the US Ambassador Robert Ford expressed concern at the strategic mistake in the airstrike campaign. During a hearing at the Committee of Foreign Affairs, he explained that the 'airstrike campaign which we started in September has actually hurt the moderate opposition. It has discredited them on the street, because our strikes targeted territory taken by the al-Qaida affiliated Nusra Front which

---

[12] Baudouin Loos, 'Les décapitations, le piège sournois des djihadistes', *Le Soir*, 15 September 2014.

has been fighting against the Assad regime . . . In fact, what we did is we played the role of the Assad air force.'[13]

It is increasingly difficult to be heard above the noise, and 'moderates' are harder to find. The *New Yorker* star cartoonist Andy Borowitz illustrated the US administration's dilemma in a cartoon showing the 'registration form for Syrian moderates'. Candidates are asked to tick one of the following boxes: A) Moderate B) Very moderate C) Crazily moderate D) Other. Many commentators have argued that there are no moderates any more, no more people worthy of trust, a point deconstructed by Thomas Pierret, who says: 'There remain a large number of reasonable people we could support, including non-jihadi Islamist groups. It would not be wrong to do so if this were included in a politically coherent strategy. To be clear: we cannot ask them to fight Islamic State while at the same time telling them we're not interested in their struggle against Assad. To be labelled "pro-Western" is today a mark of infamy among Syrian rebels, not because of a rabid hostility towards Westerners, but due to the latter's unimaginable cynicism in their management of the Syrian conflict.'

It is worth remembering that the moderates are the only ones who have ever succeeded in doing what Western air strikes and even the regime failed to do: make Islamic State lose ground. Between the end of 2013 and early 2014, the Free Syrian Army, allied with several Islamist groups, pushed Islamic State to withdraw to its strongholds of Raqqa and Deir ez-Zor. International military people keep trying to explain this, since it is hard to imagine a military operation succeeding, whatever the power ratio on the ground and the means deployed, if there is no political plan to go with it. The West itself cruelly lacks any political blueprint. The air campaign against Islamic State should have been accompanied by similar strikes against the regime and support for the opposition. Without those, it was obvious that the regime would fill the vacuum.

Ayman Abdel-Nour told me that 'when you study the threat, you must be scientific. Where is the illness? If you treat the illness, the rest of the body will heal as a matter of course. The regime is the structure that has conceived, nurtured and enabled the development of Islamic State. It is the regime that is the source of this phenomenon. We need to treat the illness. If we get rid of it, the rest will be fixed.'

Our military operation is doing the opposite: fuelling radicalism as I described previously, first through the Dabiq prophecy, then by driving Iraqi and Syrian Sunnis into the arms of jihadist ideology. This is all the more so since one of the coalition's mistakes was to bomb all jihadist groups, not just Islamic State. While Jabhat al-Nusra and Ahrar ash-Sham had at best rivalrous relations with IS (and at times openly hostile), these air raids have made them close ranks with them by designating the West as a common enemy. Jabhat al-Nusra's reaction is significant. Having been targeted by the bombings, it immediately began to dislodge the Western-backed 'moderates' from their north-western strongholds. How then to explain to Islamic Front fighters that the West still wants Bashar al-Assad to fall, while it limits itself to striking groups opposed to the dictator? The communiqué from the Syrian presidency after the first US air raids on Syrian territory was truly Machiavellian. It announced that the Pentagon had warned Assad about the bombings. It is likely that this communiqué is a lie for the media (the US certainly denied forewarning Damascus), but its effect has been devastating: the Syrian regime gave its people the impression that it was collaborating with the West. Following this apparent convergence between Washington and Damascus, the Sunnis have closed ranks, often around the strongest group: Islamic State.

And yet the vast majority of Syrians, even Sunni Arabs who have nowhere to turn, still view Islamic State as an occupation force with religious practices very different from their own *wasati* (moderate) ones, and whose doctrine shocks local populations. Despite everything, Western air strikes have greatly altered Syrians' attitudes to Islamic State. Thomas Pierret says, 'notwithstanding its capacity to re-establish order, appreciated (at least temporarily) by those who had suffered from the drift into crime of some rebel factions, IS used to be largely reviled for its sectarianism and its dedication to fighting other rebels while sparing the regime. Things have radically changed since summer 2014, when Islamic State emerged both as the regime's ruthless enemy, particularly with the seizure of the military bases in Raqqa province, and as the victim of Western powers whose cynicism is boundless, since they keep their bombs for Islamic State while they watch Assad's planes fly next to them and kill dozens of civilians with barrel-bombs on a daily basis.'

Even if the United States is often criticised for its political mistakes, there are wise people there who often sound the alarm. In mid-November 2014, Secretary of State John Kerry realised the need to 'handle' the regime at the same time as Islamic State: 'Assad and ISIL are symbiotic,' Kerry said. 'ISIL presents itself as the only alternative to Assad. Assad purports to be the last line of defence against ISIL. Both are stronger as a result.'[14] From early September, American intelligence warned the forces on the ground that military intervention was having a direct effect on the number of jihadists travelling to Syria and Iraq, and that the flow was higher than ever.

Moreover, even though the modern weapons used by Western air forces are remarkably precise, no military intervention happens without civilian losses, which army spokesmen hide under the euphemism 'collateral damage'. By 12 November 2014, the Syrian Observatory for Human Rights had recorded fifty civilian deaths in allied bombings since the air strikes began. Among them were eight children. Their photographs were on social networks in no time, where they joined pictures of Bashar al-Assad's victims and fed the dubious narrative of a great anti-Muslim coalition that had the shameful backing of several Gulf countries.

All this is a godsend for jihadist propaganda, which is now disseminated worldwide. As Romain Caillet points out, 'before the coalition's offensive, Islamic State had two branches, in Iraq and Syria. It now has five additional ones, in Egypt, Libya, Yemen, Algeria and Saudi Arabia.'

In the small Istanbul apartment where he has found refuge, the Syrian intellectual Yassin al-Haj Saleh found it hard to describe our mistakes. When I asked him what the West could do to remedy the situation, he looked at the sky, then put his head in his hands and sighed in despair. He remained silent for a while. 'It is too late. Far too late. Much, much, much too late. The West is one of the engineers of our disaster. It is responsible for our woes, at least as much as Russia and Iran. No, really, Western policy bears considerable responsibility.

---

[14] Speech in Washington on 16 November.

What we have realised too late is that the West has only one interest: security, what it calls the struggle against terrorism. It is in complete denial about the reality of our revolution.'

Instead of analysing Islamic State's strengths and weaknesses factually, we fall for its insidious propaganda by considering it evil incarnate. We surrender to easy anathema and provide Islamic State with propaganda points, rather than thinking about exposing and denouncing its contradictions. Alireza Doostdar, a Professor of Religion at Chicago University, underlines our failings in an article with the provocative title 'How not to understand ISIS': 'Our knowledge of ISIS is extremely scant. We know close to nothing about ISIS's social base. We know little about how it made its military gains, and even less about the nature of the coalitions into which it has entered with various groups—from other Islamist rebels in Syria to secular Ba'athists in Iraq.'[15]

Syrians, meanwhile, even if they suffer from Islamic State violence on a daily basis, know how to put Islamic State in context. Ayman Abdel-Nour asks bluntly: 'Why am I not afraid of Islamic State taking control of Syria? Because the population will not accept it. Islamic State will never have popular support. And our geography will not allow Islamic State to hide.'

---

[15] Alireza Dootstar, 'How Not To Understand Isis', University of Chicago. Published online on https://divinity.uchicago.edu/sightings/how-not-understand-isis-alireza-dootstar.

# 9

# Restoring Ties

*People's trust needs to be regained. The priority must be the protection of civilians.*

*Think local. Do not forget the economy. Reform governance.*

Islamic State can seem very powerful. Up to now, it has done very well when it comes to propaganda, recruitment and its approach to the Syrian regime and local tribes. But it would be a mistake to think of it as invincible—or even to imagine it is particularly strong. There are many splits and fissures within it, as well as between it and the populations it now controls, and sooner or later this will bring about its end. Either due to the radicalism of its religious diktats (prohibiting tobacco will count against it in countries where addiction to smoking is a common health problem), or because of the violence with which it exercises power, Islamic State will one day be considered unbearable by local people who will reject it as an alien transplant.

At the risk of appearing provocative, I would like to bring up the principles set out by David Galula, one of the French theorists of anti-insurgency war, forgotten in his own country and rediscovered in the United States by General David Petraeus. This book suggests that to be victorious in an asymmetrical conflict, hearts and minds must be won over. And ultimately, between the different sides in a conflict, the winner is generally the one who can give the people a sense of security. If Syrians have the impression—rightly or wrongly—of being bombed by the West, then they will hate the West. If they have the impression that Islamic State contributes to their stability, then they will reach out to Islamic State.

To involve local people, regain their trust despite our years of contempt, to have them understand that we stand by their side to fight all forms of tyranny: this is the way to win people's support. Ayman Abdel-Nour insisted to me that 'the only solution is political. The only absolute given is that Bashar must not be part of the solution. There must be guarantees for minorities, and the whole of society will cure itself. The first stage must be a political agreement. The day this agreement is struck, Islamic State will lose half its members. In a single day! Because all we need is fresh hope!'

Once this hope returns, part of the solution could come from the Sahwas, tribal militias on the Iraqi model. But again, we are doing things the wrong way round. We support or secure support from (from Saudi Arabia in the case of Islamic Front, Turkey for Jamal Maarouf's movement)—and only with money—men and groups who don't always possess the necessary legitimacy. Ayman Abdel-Nour stresses 'the Sahwas can only come during a second stage'. Islamic State first of all needs to be stripped of it attraction to recruits. On the other hand, 'the raids against Islamic State are the fulfilment of President Obama's admission: we have no plan and no strategy. They amount to providing complete immunity for Bashar al-Assad. They only serve Bashar, strengthening him and weakening the moderates.'

The bad news, in these times of slashed budgets, is that, if indeed we resort to Sahwas, we Westerners will probably have to pay for them. We have seen that regional players—and Muslim donors in general—are very worried about the Syrians' fate. They have already donated a great deal of money to finance humanitarian action or organisations for the support of human rights, or directly to arm fighting units. The problem is that each country—Turkey, Saudi Arabia, Qatar—has its own agenda and wants to extend its regional influence.

The failed states of Afghanistan and Iraq provide every opportunity for neighbouring countries to apply policies aimed at gaining influence at a low cost. The vacuum is so easy to fill that the temptation is great for bordering nations to use a failed state's territory as a 'playground' for war by proxy. Such a process is of course destructive, but the maxim 'who pays the piper calls the tune' is well known. We cannot run the risk of seeing countries in the region, for example, making connections with or recruiting local armed groups, and giving them suitcases filled with dollars with the sole instruction, 'take this and kill Shias'.

The least bad solution in Syria is perhaps the worst in Iraq. Amnesty International advisor Donatella Rovera is irritated by the Sahwa 'fashion' in Iraq, a country where the United States is looking to repeat its 2007–08 successes. State Department officials have therefore been pressing Baghdad to adopt a law on the National Guard as soon as possible. Rovera says that this is 'nothing more than a project to create a new Sahwa—yet another militia. Everybody swears by them as the only solution, but I fail to see how the Sahwas could be the answer. At the time of the original Sahwas, there was a political dynamic. Now there is nothing. Sahwas shouldn't be created because the army and police aren't doing their jobs protecting the population. That's the problem that needs solving, rather than creating a new militia, which will operate outside legal frameworks.

Rather than solving the problem, this creates new ones.' She therefore strongly recommends a complete restructuring of the army and police, and a rooting out of sectarianism in these institutions, rather than a proliferation of militias.

Ultimately some degree of intervention is inevitable, though the very word 'intervention' has been cursed since George Bush's invasions of Afghanistan and Iraq. And anyone who thinks al-Qaida was punished for the 9/11 attacks when the United States responded by forming coalitions to conquer these two countries is very naïve indeed.

The strength of resistance to intervention has been pronounced in recent years, from anti-militarist and pro-Third World movements as well as defenders of sovereignty. Yet it is a fact that our Western armed forces are currently involved in Iraq and to an extent in Syria. Can we bear to see American and Canadian bombers crossing the path of Assad's helicopters over Syria, while these very helicopters drop their TNT barrels on Aleppo? Can we accept that we do nothing, since this is not our pilots' mission (which is solely to fight Islamic State), and that protecting civilians is not part of their mandate? It is hard not to think, when you see the air raids carried out by the Syrian Air Force—such as the one on 25 November 2014, over civilian areas of Raqqa, which killed more than a hundred people and destroyed a large part of the city's museum, which even the mujahadin had not dared to touch—that these raids could not be executed without at least the tacit Pentagon approval. In any case, the US Air Force certainly saw the planes take off, and decided to let them go ahead. An opposition activist based in Antakya in Turkey, quoted by *Le Monde* correspondent Benjamin Barthe, asked, 'How could the regime send its planes to a city over which the American air force flies permanently, without seeking US permission?' Another activist in Antakya, Ward am-Raqqawi, was quoted in the same interview: 'American and Syrian warplanes fly over our heads at a few hours' interval. On Tuesday afternoon, it was the Syrians, and on Tuesday evening, the Americans. No aerial ballet like this can be orchestrated without coordination.' As we have seen (and as Galula says), the protection of civilians is key in asymmetrical warfare. If we do not protect them because it is the moral thing to do, we should at least do so out of self-interest.

So what should we do? Establish a minimal no-fly zone? Soldiers, and specialists in international law, will respond that a no-fly zone already constitutes war. So what? Are we not already involved in war operations? From a legal viewpoint, is the US Air Force not already violating Syrian air space on a daily basis? If a Syrian Air Force helicopter were downed by a Western fighter jet immediately after bombing a civilian area, would the message not be powerful enough to deter the regime from pursuing its war crimes? Would the legitimacy of such an act of war not be easy to defend against possible indictment under international law?

It is even possible to imagine a limited military operation, which would not necessarily involve great resources, as its aim would be to stay as focused as possible on the protection of civilians. Relevant to this operation would be, for instance, destroying a tank that fired on a civilian area, or bombing a base that housed militias who carried out raids on the population. This military involvement would only work in tandem with an effort to arm and support the Free Syrian Army. Finally, as emphasised by Ayman Abdel-Nour, a political process is needed, as well as assertive political backing for the forces that have struggled for four years for a democratic Syria. The last three years have led revolutionaries to water down their demands. The positions are no longer so irreconcilable. Many of them now accept the idea of a dialogue with Russia, and some even with Iran. The revolution is ready for concessions if power ends up in the hands of the Syrian people.

Power for the Syrians is all that Bassam al-Ahmad of the Violations Documentation Center asks: 'Civil society groups which are trying to rebuild the country also need support. Humanitarian refugee zones also need to be created.' He also argues for dialogue to defuse sectarian escalation: 'Diplomacy is needed. Everyone needs to speak to each other. Negotiation is paramount. Even Iran, even Hezbollah, have to be included, in order to understand what they want and what they fear, and to reassure them. It is very important to reassure minorities and for everyone to talk together.'

Riad Seif has a readymade plan for a political transition: 'Syrians themselves have been excluded from the decision-making process. There's always a lot of talk about Assad or the opposition leaders in exile who take away people's right to speak. No one represents the Syrians! But they are the real power which has to be activated. We must find a way to create a mechanism to establish a truly representative council, and not something like Etilaf [the Coalition] or the Syrian Nation Council.' The ex-MP suggests the creation of a representative transitional council, which would have seven members, to represent all Syrian religious and ethnic communities. 'There are people who can attract consensus. Ali Habib (the ex-Defence Minister, now a refugee in France) would be an acceptable delegate for the Alawis, and for the rest of the population too. Among the Kurds and the Christians, there are several people from civil society who are very respectable and could also be accepted. The same is true of the Sunnis, secularists and conservatives.'

This solution looks very similar to what General Petraeus put in place in Mosul after Saddam Hussein's downfall; and we have seen its limits. The other problem is that the regime is very unlikely to accept any political solution. The same is probably true of Islamic State. Riad Seif believes that 'this is why all of the international community's weight and pressure will be needed to constrain these players.'

The solution to the regional crisis will inevitably involve the grassroots. And it should not overlook the economy. In fact, it could start there. The French-Syrian journalist Hala Kodmani told me, 'There are models of collective management in certain neighbourhoods and certain villages, particularly in the region of Idlib, but also in Aleppo, which are very creative.' She added admiringly: 'There is a breath of life that does not want to die!' She described her encounters, in particular with women who were painting basements to refurbish schools and try to bring children back into class, often after a gap of three years. She spoke of efforts to restart local economies in areas liberated from the regime. Assistance with setting up micro-businesses and cooperatives is sometimes much more efficient than a huge humanitarian operation. Syrian women are a wonderful asset, and should not be overlooked.

Finally, the involvement of Syrian businessmen could enable the creation of a new dynamic. These businessmen still own substantial fortunes. Some are already part of the opposition and are funding media outlets or armed groups from abroad. However, most are still waiting; they do not want to burn their bridges as long as the deadlock continues—they are waiting for a signal before becoming more involved. Ayman Abdel-Nour told me that 'all the businessmen are ready and waiting for the day of reconstruction. All they want is to be able to come back and invest in their country's future.' In Jihad Yazigi's view, 'Syrian businessmen, but also Lebanese ones, are all waiting for reconstruction. But that won't happen with Bashar in power, because of the sanctions.'

# 10

# Understanding Islamic State

*Islamic State is as much a sect as a terrorist group.*

*There must be a way out for those disillusioned with jihad.*

*Why not a 'legal jihad'?*

People often complain that we lack the keys to understanding Islamic State. The media and politicians keep bringing up the same anathemas and clichés. Yet Islamic State is simply implementing a political programme devised ten years ago, disseminated in jihadist forums and translated into several languages. The author of this programme was one Abu Bakr al-Naji, a Saudi, judging by his nom de guerre. His manifesto is entitled *Management of Savagery: The Most Critical Stage Through Which the Islamic Nation Will Pass.* The plan is uncompromising: it consists of exploiting the authoritarian nature of Arab regimes and using this against them, as in martial arts, where the principle is to turn the enemy's strength—in this case, violence—against him. As Michael Weiss and Hassan Hassan have explained, Abu Bakr al-Naji 'conceived a battle plan for weakening the enemy states through what he called "power of vexation and exhaustion"'. He 'was using the time-honored jihadist example of Egypt, but he was also implicitly referring to Iraq. Here he urged the rapid consolidation of jihadist victory in order to "take over the surrounding countries".'[1]

By making use of local frustrations, propaganda and political violence among the people, the aim is to provoke an escalation of savagery. States will respond with even more violence and eventually governments will lose all legitimacy in the eyes of the ruled. Amid the chaos, jihadists intervene by presenting themselves as an alternative to the state's failure. In his research, the political consultant Frantz Glasman describes Islamic State's modus operandi: 'By re-establishing security, restarting social services, and taking charge of the administration of territories, they can manage this chaos, following a Hobbesian pattern of state building. With the extension of the "territories of chaos", regions administered by the jihadists will multiply, forming the core of their future caliphate. Whether persuaded or not, the populations under their control will accept this Islamic governance.'[2]

This theory of political violence is in one way quite standard. It has much in common with what nihilist theorists seek, but also with the practices of radical groups in many other countries. Yet it is unique in jihadi terms, in that it clearly distances itself from al-Qaida's methods. Al-Qaida concentrates

---

[1] Michael Weiss and Hassan Hassan 2014, Ibid. The authors add that they were told by one ISIS affiliated cleric that Naji's 'book is widely circulated among provincial ISIS commanders and some rank-and-file fighters as a way to justify beheadings as not only religiously permissible but recommended by God and his Prophet'.

[2] Frantz Glasman, 'Vie locale et concurrence de projets politiques dans les territoires sous contrôle de l'opposition, des djihadistes et des Kurdes en Syrie'. (Local life and competition of political projects in the territories held by the opposition, jihadists and the Kurds in Syria.)

on the 'distant enemy', the West, often described as Israel's proxy. Most salient of all, it claims no territory, at least not in the short term.

By contrast, Islamic State focuses on the enemy nearby. For the youths now fighting in Syria, the Shia are a much more immediate enemy than the Christians or Jews (the targets of al-Qaida, whose original name was 'World Islamic Front for Jihad against the Jews and Crusaders'). Islamic State's slogan is: 'Nine bullets for apostates, one for Crusaders.' Its strategy consists in taking advantage of a state's failures, trying to provoke and hasten its demise, in order to seize a failed territory and force itself on the people living there.

Both in style and PR, the difference between Islamic State and al-Qaida is striking. The emergence of Islamic State will have made many aware of the fact that al-Qaida is a movement for the better off. Osama bin Laden was a billionaire and the scion of a great family. He was educated and travelled to the West. Abu Musab al-Zarqawi comes from a family of refugees and spent his childhood in one of the ugliest, most squalid and polluted cities in Jordan. Bin Laden was the offspring of the Saudi equivalent of the Rockefellers. He spoke to the bourgeoisie, to rich and reactionary donors of the Gulf. Zarqawi speaks to the Middle East's children in the street, but also to those in the West. When bin Laden had a message for the world, he would take pains to record it, developing his points at length, replete with religious and political references, and setting out the detail of his worldview. When Zarqawi delivered his first message from Iraq in 2004, he appeared knife in hand. After a few muttered words, he beheaded his hostage, Nicholas Berg, then posted the footage on YouTube, in a video that lasted just a few seconds. Zarqawi's ideology is reduced to its simplest form.

There is no lenghty exposition of theory. It's as if there is no message apart from violence.

Frantz Glasman points out, however, the difficulties faced by Islamic State in administering territories it has seized out of chaos without the caliphate collapsing because of failures of governance or resistance from armed opponents (of the Sahwa type, created in reaction to IS terror). A document published in 2010 focused on strengthening the 'Islamic State of Iraq', and set out principles that would enable the caliphate to last.

It emphasised the importance of uniting Islamic State's potential constituency (Sunni Arabs) and avoiding becoming remote from them. To do so, terror policies—which work when taking control initially and eliminating potential rivals—need to be replaced with effective administration. The caliphate must prioritise providing people with basic public services and security. Of course, the more violent and sectarian the common enemy, the more readily this narrative of cohesion will be accepted. Syria's Assad and Iraq's Abadi are partners of choice in Islamic State's agenda. And President Sisi in Egypt shows excellent potential too.

From a military viewpoint, terror is a weapon. It is not enough just to kill an enemy, be they a Shia, Kurd, Iraqi soldier or Syrian revolutionary. The enemy's body must be desecrated. He must be beheaded and crucified. And above all, filmed. The victim must be recorded and the images disseminated as widely as possible. Horror aims to demoralise the enemy, wither his motivation, break up his ranks, cause desertion. There is little doubt that the Iraqis who abandoned their positions and relinquished Mosul to the jihadists had Islamic State's atrocities in mind, which they would have seen on the Internet. The jihadist document quotes Sun Tzu, author of *The Art of War*, when they describe a 'scorched earth policy'. The ancient

Chinese strategist recommended giving priority to hit-and-run tactics, which are less costly and more effective than pitched battles. He also advocated maintaining unceasing pressure on the enemy through constant harassment, particularly the assassination of prominent figures.

Islamic State has drawn its own conclusions from the Sahwas established by the US in Iraq. It has seen their formidable effectiveness: in just two years, they all but eradicated al-Qaida in Iraq. But Islamic State is also aware that the tribes mobilised by the Americans fought Zarqawi for pecuniary rather than political ends. US funding has corrupted and largely criminalised these 'awakening' councils. Islamic State has called for repurposing the concept of Sahwas for its own aims, taking the initiative in arming the tribes and joining them with their own struggle, before the Iraqi government decides to do so again. To ensure the tribes' loyalty Islamic State offers them devolved authority, in doing so making them their local proxies.[3] This disengagement would free Islamic State fighters up for other duties, save the group's resources, and ensure their new partners' allegiance.

Romain Caillet got a lot of attention in the media when he suggested that Islamic State had made al-Qaida 'untrendy'. And this is key. Islamic State transforms jihad into a product of globalisation loaded with strong Western connotations.

---

[3] As described by Pierre-Jean Luizard in *Le piège Daech: L'Etat Islamique ou le retour de l'histoire*, when he mentions how IS consolidates its hold, by 'resting on the delegation of power to local players, as opposed to what al-Qaida has done. A delegation that is not merely formal: in Falloujah and in Mosul, very shortly after the city's conquest, militiamen belonging to the Islamic State have withdrawn from the city centre to settle at the periphery and defend the edges of town.'

Islamic State's power is spreading the idea among our lost youth that 'jihad is cool'. While al-Qaida followers are steeped in a Middle Eastern culture, with strong regional references, Islamic State members are products of Facebook and Twitter.

The way they hijacked the hashtag #Ferguson during the riots in the United States, to spread (not unironically) the message among Afro-Americans that the Koran stands for racial equality, shows their skill in manipulating social networks. They are also very adept at subverting attempts at counter-narrative. They like challenging the US State Department's Twitter account (@Thinkagain_DOS), showing up its contradictions, often clumsily but sometimes with real humour.

Islamic State jihadists are fans of *LOLcats*. They call themselves the *Fanboys*. They all have watched *Game of Thrones*, *Lord of the Rings* and *Harry Potter*. Several told me that they see parallels with their own struggle in the movie *The Matrix*. Some have trained for combat by playing the videogame *Call of Duty*. One of my most sadistic jailers, who was British, was also a *Simpsons* fan. Others even see in the way beheadings are filmed allusions to the reality TV show *Top Chef*.

To justify violence, they point out on social networks that we are not living in a world of fairy tales and teddy bears (or, in the case of English-speaking Islamic State militants, Tellytubbies). Mehdi Nemmouche, who murdered four people in Brussels' Jewish Museum, whistled the theme from the French children's programme *Club Dorothée*. This is all the stranger when you consider that once in Syria or Iraq with Islamic State, fighters are prohibited from watching TV and listening to music, activities considered *haram* and forbidden by religion. The result is that most devote themselves to singing *nashid*, hymns remixed with special effects, with an undeniably hypnotic effect. I remember listening for hours to 'Dawlat al-

Islam Qamat' ('The Islamic State has been founded') or 'Nahnu ansar ash-Sharia' ('We are the companions of Sharia'), played over and over on my captors' computers or mobile phones . . . These obsessive tunes are designed to stick in your head.

Many jihadists are mediocre Muslims and many are fresh converts, or recent returnees to the faith. They compensate for being newcomers to the faith with extraordinary radicalism. The French parliamentarian Patrick Menucci explained that 'from work conducted by the state, the Direction Générale de la Sécurité Extérieure (DGSE, French foreign intelligence) and NGOs, we know that across a group of 120 families whose children left for jihad with Daesh, 70 per cent are atheists and 80 per cent have no link, even a distant one, with immigration. Out of 650 calls received by a French hotline for reporting radicalised people who have been radicalised as part of a government anti-jihad programme, 55 per cent are from families of Arab-Moslem origin, and 45 per cent are from families of different cultures and religions.'[4]

Maha Yahya, a researcher at the Carnegie Middle East Center, is the author of an article entitled 'The Ultimate Fatal Attraction: The Five Reasons People Join ISIS'.[5] She lists, in order of importance, (i) the failure of school systems, (ii) the lack of economic opportunity, which is related to (iii) the population pyramid and poor economic growth, (iv) bad governance of states in the region, linked finally to (v) the loss of people's

[4] General discussion of the law proposal of Philippe Meunier, on 26 November 2014, during the examination by the Commission of Constitutional Laws, of Legislation and General Administration of the Republic.

[5] http://carnegie-mec.org/2014/11/07/ultimate-fatal-attraction-5-reasons-people-join-isis.

trust because of dictatorship and authoritarianism. The Arab Spring (or as she calls it, the 'Arab Awakening') has worsened the situation, against a background of a loss of confidence in the West (with huge disappointment over the actions of Western countries). Arabs have come to the point where they systematically attribute dark motives to the West, akin to conspiracy theories, criticising both its interventions when they do take place, and its inaction when they don't.

Yahya does not follow her argument all the way through. The social, economic and political reasons she describes as favouring Islamic State are in fact also the main motivators of the Arab Spring itself. How the state reacts determines whether a rebellion produces democracy or a descent into violence. As Arab regimes allowed no place for dissent, peaceful opposition did not stand a chance in Syria or in many other Middle Eastern countries. Western support for these regimes is the main reason for the region's loss of trust in the West. We cannot re-establish links without clearly distancing ourselves from dictatorial governments.

I have a friend who works as a consultant for USAID, the US Agency for International Development. He recently described his disillusionment to me: 'Americans have excellent experts who've long understood why crises happen, and have excellent ideas for solving them. The problem is when these explanations get to the top. No one wants to listen. As soon as you go beyond the prevailing orthodoxy, the most intelligent reasoning becomes inaudible.'

Many aspects of French sociologist Olivier Roy's analysis of the social and psychological reasons for the commitment of Islamic State jihadists are worth heeding. In an interview with the French weekly *L'Express*, Roy explained after the publication of his book *En quête de l'Orient perdu* ('In

Search of the Lost Orient') that 'we are facing generational nihilism, a youth fascinated by death. This phenomenon is expressed through risky behaviours, overdoses, an attraction to Satanism … In some cases a pathological breeding ground for morbidness. In the case of Islamic State, as with globalisation's lost children, who are frustrated or on society's margins, they feel invested with a sense of omnipotence, because of their own violence, which in addition they see as legitimate.'[6]

Roy adds that 'Islamic State provides them with a real battle ground where they can find fulfilment. That is their stroke of genius. They can take in many more volunteers than al-Qaida, which recruits secretly. Now, jihadists can fight openly to defend a territory as part of a jihadist battalion. They feel like heroes in pre-planned videos in which they explain why they are happy to die as martyrs.' This scholarly view was put more prosaically by an American intelligence source (nicknamed 'Richard'), who, in an interview with Michael Weiss, described these young volunteers for jihad as 'knucklehead nineteen-year-olds looking to do something in their life because they don't have shit to do back in Belgium'.[7]

The interpretative tools conventionally used when discussing sectarian phenomena are particularly well suited to analysing the cases of individuals who join Islamic State. The process often begins with what the people involved describe as a 'life accident', often a serious family conflict, a relationship break-up or the realisation that they have been living a 'bad life' through

[6] Olivier Roy, 'Les jeunes djihadistes sont des suicidaires', *L'Express*, 3 November 2014.

[7] Michael Weiss and Hassan Hassan, *Isis: Inside the army of terror*, Regan Arts, 2014.

involvement in crime, for example. Exposure to ultra-violence on social media contributes to a sense of vulnerability, lack of judgment, and ultimately to the conditioning which will later make them susceptible to brainwashing.

Exposure to violence is something I myself witnessed and it is very disturbing. Throughout my years covering the Syrian conflict, my social networks would continuously post pictures of tortured bodies, corpses of children grey with dust being pulled from the rubble after a bombing, dismembered casualties, blood, and smoking pieces of flesh and bone. It created an accumulation of horrors, more concentrated than in any single conflict zone. In general, professionals such as journalists, aid workers and soldiers are provided with monitoring and counselling to prevent post-traumatic stress caused by such images. In the past, people were not exposed to them until after they left the front line. No front line presents the same density of horrors. Now, without warning, the Internet brings a concentration of violence far beyond what is experienced even in the bloodiest conflict zones into everyday life in the West. It is not hard to understand why this can be so destabilising. Recruiters for jihad know this and exploit it to the full.

Wannabe jihadists build a world view with little connection to reality: a vision of the universe based on the idea of a huge conspiracy of the powerful against the weak, on the concept of martyrdom of Muslims (of some Muslims, since they are very selective when it comes to defining who is a member of the Umma), and a condemnation of media narratives, which they say is always based on double standards. This vision is very hard to deconstruct because, even though it is a caricature, it is founded on a few truths and highlights some of our genuine mistakes.

John Bell, the director of the Middle East programme at the International Center for Peace in Toledo, has drawn a striking comparison between the Inquisition and Islamic State.[8] In both cases, there is the idea of *Autodafé* ('Act of faith') as a justification for crimes, as well as exclusion (*takfir*), which parallels the concept of excommunication. In both cases there is a call to persecute minorities: the Yazidis and Ismailis have replaced the Cathars[9] and Huguenots. And both use violence, torture and death to impose their fanatical and exclusive vision of religion.

To pursue this iconoclastic comparison, it is worth noting that the motives of Western volunteers who go to fight Islamic State are very similar to those who join Islamic State itself. The Facebook page 'Lions of Rojava' is the official showcase in the West for recruitment by the PYD Kurdish party. Veterans seeking recognition or blasé bikers sign up for a 'jihad' against Islamic State, side by side with Peshmerga, whose appeal to Western public opinion we have already discussed. The discourse of these 'lions' (a term found in both Islamic State and PYD propaganda) employs similar rhetoric. Indeed, their

---

[8] John Bell, 'Confidence men and their masquerade', op-ed published on the aljazeera.com website 21 September 2014.

[9] A Christian movement with many followers in the south of France in the 11th, 12th and 13th centuries. This creed believed in reincarnation and in the *Consolament* (blessing with hands placed on the forehead) instead of church communion, and denied the Catholic clergy any authority. This heresy was violently persecuted by the Inquisition and by a Crusade of the Kings of France and Aragon, until its last members were judged and sentenced. The details of the trials of Cathars can be found in Emmanuel Leroy-Ladurie's masterpiece *Montaillou, village occitan*, which uses all the written legal and historical documentation available on a particular village of southern France (translator's note).

Facebook page announces: SEND TERRORISTS TO HELL AND SAVE HUMANITY.

At the start, they probably also share the same good intentions. When they arrive, there is the same naïve commitment to a war beyond their grasp, the same promise of high adventure as revenge for a frustrating life, of some action to stave off day-to-day boredom. It is unsurprising that the political scientist Mohammed Tozy became interested in what he has called 'the romanticism of jihad'. Both jihadists and Kurdish supporters enjoy the feeling of re-enacting the Spanish Civil War, or being part of contemporary International Brigades and, of course, of being on the right side of history. They also have the same highly selective attitude when it comes to mercy. Ultimately, their fighters are subjected to similar indoctrination—though I must stress the differences between jihadists and Kurdish supporters in terms of level of criminality.

Reducing Islamic State to the status of a sect removes it from its pedestal, and dispels the notion of 'super-terrorist group' it tries so hard to create, an image that Western leaders themselves do much to spread, since most Western countries are at war with Islamic State, and the portrayal of the enemy plays a part in every war effort. The media treatment of Islamic State has just as many shortcomings. It is still extremely emotional, it casts anathema and seeks to understand neither the motivations of people who travel to fight, nor the local people's reactions to Islamic State.

Islamic State has constructed a legend and we are its eager audience. We think we can protect ourselves by not using the name it has chosen ('so-called Islamic State' and 'Daesh' are commonly used in the media) and putting a 'propaganda footage' caption at the bottom of the screen in television reports. And that is how we fall into Islamic State's trap. With this warning caption in place, which (cheaply) gets a TV channel off the hook, the most spectacular of Islamic State's carefully produced videos continue to be shown. With each new criminal spectacle, our media rush to respond to Islamic State's wish to get itself on our agenda. This happens so often that any mentally ill person knows that in order to get on TV he only needs to carry out an action while brandishing a black banner. Success is guaranteed. Romain Caillet expressed his regret in an interview given to the web newspaper *Mediapart* that 'we are in the realm of the sensational, the murky; our feelings are being played on. None of it makes any sense. I have almost never worked on French jihadists, yet most journalists who contact me do so to interview me about them.'[10]

Media sensationalism is one of the most counter-productive and self-defeating aspects of our war against Islamic State. It reflects Western fascination in unemployed youths from nondescript or, squalid European, North American or Australian neighbourhoods, who rise from professional and social limbo or a life of petty crime, to terrorist stardom via Twitter, Facebook or Instagram. Teenage boys and girls have not only felt like celebrities by joining a cause they view as romantic; they have become themselves celebrities in the Western press, even though (and perhaps especially because) they are painted as criminals joining a death cult. As Michael Weiss and Hassan Hassan write, 'Western sensationalism has perversely contributed to the lure of glamour of ISIS as much as it has to its lurid appeal to the young and disaffected.

---

[10] Romain Caillet, 'Le djihadisme n'est vu qu'au travers du sensationnel et de l'émotion' (Jihadism is only ever looked at with sensationalism and emotion), *Médiapart*, 26 November 2014.

Stories about pretty, middle-class teenage Austrian girls going off to fight with and marry the *takfiris*—and copycats who are stopped en route before they can reach Syria—continue to draw headlines in the same way as Charles Manson's latest nuptials. People are fascinated by the psychopathic spectacle of ISIS, and especially by those they see as "like them" but who are so drawn to it that they abandon seemingly comfortable lives in the West to jihadism.'[11]

The police and authorities, on the other hand, are making a big mistake when they turn young jihadis into major-league terrorists. France's first trials of returning jihadis took place in autumn 2014. The first person convicted was a convert named Flavien, who was sentenced to seven years. They made an example of him, taking into account the terrorist nature of the crimes he was found guilty of. With Islamic State recruiting left, right and centre, the court wanted to make an impression by showing that joining such a group has serious consequences. The verdict was intended as 'an example', for better or worse. Flavien appears to have been really naïve, as was clear from what he said in the dock: ' I was for al-Qaida, but against violence.' In fact, he probably did not participate in the fighting. In all, he spent just ten days in Syria. Even worse, he was there in December 2012, when Islamic State did not yet exist. If the law is applied in this way to the hundreds of French citizens who have actually fought for Islamic State, what sentences should be handed down to them? And where should these sentences be served? There is a risk of creating a French Guantanamo, along the lines suggested by French MP Nicolas Dupont-Aignan who, in a populist outburst, proposed a reopening of the penal colony in French Guyana.

[11] Michael Weiss and Hassan Hassan, *Isis: Inside the army of terror*.

One morning in October 2014, I received a message from a young man from Sion in Switzerland:

> I was an independent photographer just starting out who, after many trips to Palestine, wanted to produce some photo-journalism on Syria, which I hoped would have sufficient 'shock value' to make my name. I made contacts over there, and got in touch with (or was put in touch with) some bad people. As I had become a Muslim the previous year, these people convinced me to go to Syria, not to do journalism, but, as they put it, to do my Moslem 'jihad' by helping Syria, helping the people there, through photography or by delivering medical care in an ambulance.

This young man—I'll call him Sebastien—was picked up at the border, and was rapidly imprisoned by Islamic State supporters when he told them he planned to go home. He spent two months in Islamic State jails, transported from Aleppo to Raqqa, but was fortunate enough to be offered clemency by a *qadi* (Islamic judge), who let him leave and even returned his confiscated personal effects.[12]

This happened in spring 2014. Young men like him are no longer so lucky. Now, the journey to Syria is always a one-way ticket. Islamic State does not let people who have become disillusioned with jihad leave freely—and there are many of them. To avoid infiltration and defections, jihadists who want to go home are generally detained. Many of them are imprisoned, and some are executed. We meanwhile face a tough moral question: if we imagine a violent sect which

---

[12] He was then put on trial by the Swiss judicial system, which handed him a symbolic sentence.

forbids its members from leaving, and even threatens them with death, what steps should we take to fight it? Should we encourage deserters? Offer means of escape? Instead of this, a young person who finds himself caught up in a jihadist adventure he regrets is faced with all sorts of hurdles: from the group holding him, and the knowledge that if he manages to escape from Syria, he will be thrown into jail, probably for a long time. If 'deradicalisation' (to use that ghastly new term) is the aim, there are better ways of going about it. In fact, these disillusioned young people are probably our best allies in our struggle against indoctrination.

To prevent radicalisation, rather than putting imams on Arab dictators' payrolls, we could seek to channel the goodwill of all those (Muslims and others) who are shocked by crimes committed in Syria and who simply wonder: 'How can I help?' We could devise some sort of 'legal jihad' to stop more young people ending up in the clutches of terrorists. We could promote humanitarian, social and other types of engagement. As far as I know, no such programme exists.

In addition, such an initiative would allow Muslims to reclaim the term 'jihad', which has been corrupted by extremists and hijacked by the Western media. Jihad—and this is something that we tend to forget—was initially one of Islam's most beautiful concepts. It is the effort, exerted on and for oneself, with the aim of becoming better, improving one's life and striving for a fairer world.

Our young people, whom we often describe as lacking values, of being individualistic and materialistic, deserve opportunities to commit themselves to something better than criminal gangs.

# Conclusion—A New State
# of Barbarity

Islamic State's success stems from a number of our mistakes. It is the result of the improbable cross-fertilisation between two groups the scholar François Burgat has rightly called 'jihadists without borders' and 'angry Sunnis'. The two met in Iraq and Syria and created an ideal, yet largely fantasised 'Sunnistan'.[1] In the minds of the jihadists lies a real identity crisis, the feeling of being

> outcasts from the political systems of the countries they come from [...] The mechanisms of radicalism [in the West], which are triggered in a small number of individuals, are not purely economic and social, nor purely religious. They are above all political. The angst and discontent of many Muslims, both young and old, not only reflects the real difficulties of professional integration in those communities, and the individuals in them often globally (and lazily) described as 'the youth of the *banlieues*'. This discontent, which surfaces

[1] François Burgat, 'Djihadistes sans frontières, pourquoi ils partent en guerre' (Jihadism without borders: why they go to war), *OrientXXI. info*, 27 October 2014.

among Muslims even when they distance themselves from this schismatic and disruptive behaviour, has even fewer links with their supposedly good or bad interpretation of Islamic dogma. It requires a straightforwardly political analysis.[2]

The mechanics of radicalisation operate on two different levels. At the individual level, they are set in motion as a result of failed integration and identity-based narratives that produce social exclusion. At the diplomatic level, by the West's prioritisation of autocrats over their people. Europe and the United States' attitude to Marshal Abdel-Fattah Sisi is an indication that we have not learned the key lesson of the Arab Spring. The idea still holds sway in our political establishment that dictatorships can be an effective bulwark against extremism. As we have seen, and as we know, the opposite is the case. Dictatorships provide breeding ground and fuel for extremism.

Why such blindness? Thomas Pierret suggests:

> If you want to be charitable, you could say that it is faulty analysis which mistakes a poison for its antidote, in other words, sees regimes that have enabled extremism to take root by blocking legal forms of political participation as a bulwark. A more severe assessment would suggest that part of Western public opinion is only ready to allow Arabs the right to vote if the results in the ballot boxes favour the parties which meet all our demands, i.e. parties which are pro-Western, secular and economically liberal.

We Westerners regularly boast about setting a good example. We like to see ourselves as models of development,

[2] Ibid.

civilisation and democracy. It is this kind of thinking which fed nineteenth-century left-wing colonialism. Except that in Syria, we do have to admit that we have seen individual initiatives, which are lessons in courage and commitment. Syrians have been remarkable and incredibly imaginative in their attempts to invent democratic structures, despite the repression.

Though few have heard of him, Omar Aziz, an economist educated in Grenoble in France, is one of the revolution's heroes. He returned to Syria when the revolution broke out. He is considered the founder of local coordination committees. He was arrested by the ruthless Air Force Intelligence Services and died after three months of torture. The Syrian revolution is full of this kind of heroism. It is our duty to pay homage to the memory of such brave individuals by not forgetting the Syrian people, their suffering and courage. Yet who in the West remembers Omar Aziz?

History is cruel; it is more likely to remember the names of the villains than the heroes. Our security fixation has led us to make shameful compromises. Whereas the American military air intervention in Iraq and Syria alone costs ten million dollars a day, the United Nations' World Food Program in the winter of 2014/15 had to interrupt its delivery of food to Syrian refugees because of lack of funding. The millions of Syrians living in makeshift camps on their country's borders were forced to spend the winter with empty stomachs.

How then can we be surprised that our indifference causes anger and a loss of trust and credibility? Like Yassin al-Haj Saleh, an increasing number of Syrians who are both democratic and secular have lost any respect they may have had for the West. One of my friends from Raqqa recently said: 'We shall not die in silence. We've been shouting for three years and you refuse to listen to us.' Jihad Yazigi admits that for him, 'it has been clear for quite some time that the West does not want the regime to fall. The conflict is stuck in both directions. The opposition has no hope of taking a major city. The army has no way of retaking the Ghouta or the lost countryside. This is a situation that the West likes. The only thing it is bothered about is that it would rather Bashar hadn't done so much killing, as that would make it easier to support him like it supports Sisi in Egypt.'

We do nevertheless have to care about Syria and Iraq. These countries are Europe's neighbours. If we forget them, they will remind us of their existence in the worst possible way: through images of violence and via terrorist attacks. Demonstrations of their despair will return to blow up in our faces. We should also bear in mind the strength and resilience of Syrians. Hala Kodmani suggests that 'their best form of resistance is not men under arms. It is that of civilians, of those who continue to find the strength to burst out laughing from the depths of hideouts and basements, caught between regime bombings and jihadist checkpoints.' Yet how much longer can laughter survive? The political scientist Hamit Bozarslan is worried that 'the Arab city, the Arab body politic, is dying. It could well be that in 2020 there will be no Syrian society, no Iraqi society, and no Yemeni society either. I am not sure that everybody realises how serious the situation is.'[3]

[3] Lecture given on 30 November 2014.

# Acknowledgements

My thanks go to all the Iraqis and Syrians I met during the last twelve years of reporting. They spoke to me though it sometimes put their lives at risk, and always showed disarming hospitality and kindness. I owe them my understanding of their country and their society. They contributed to discarding old clichés we like to delude ourselves with when speaking of the Orient, an area we often describe as 'complicated'.

I would like to extend my immense gratitude to those who helped me with the writing of this book, sharing their thoughts and enabling me to take advantage of their expert knowledge. I would also like to thank all those who agreed to my requests for interviews carried out for this book. Their contribution was essential. Wladimir and Frantz Glasman provided me with particularly noteworthy assistance. Martin Makinson was not only in charge of the translation into English, but also provided me with many updates and details on Iraq and Syria, a country which he lived and worked in for many years until the outbreak of the revolution. His proficiency on the geography and history of Syria was particularly useful in understanding the Jazira, a region where he worked as an archaeologist in the 1990s and 2000s. Of course I am solely responsible for any errors that may remain in the text.

Finally, I must pay tribute to all the victims of these conflicts. It would be unfair to draw up a complete list, since it is impossible to be comprehensive and I would lose myself in an inappropriate ordering of casualties. I would however like to express my immense sympathy for Paolo Dall'Oglio, a Jesuit priest who, like me, has 'Syria in his heart'. A month after my abduction, he went to Raqqa to negotiate a truce between jihadists and Kurdish fighters. When he arrived at the seat of the governorate to request an audience from the Islamic State emir, he also had in mind the names of a number of hostages detained by the group, whose release he was hoping to obtain. I was one of these hostages. In the end, he was himself captured. Now that I have come out of Islamic State jails and he is still missing, I would like to express my eternal gratitude to him.

# Index

*Note:* The letter 'n' following locators refers to notes respectively.

148    Index